CW00404228

# *on track ...*
# Pearl Jam

## every album, every song

Ben L. Connor

sonicbondpublishing.com

Sonicbond Publishing Limited
www.sonicbondpublishing.co.uk
Email: info@sonicbondpublishing.co.uk

First Published in the United Kingdom 2022
First Published in the United States 2022

British Library Cataloguing in Publication Data:
A Catalogue record for this book is available from the British Library

Copyright Ben L. Connor 2022

ISBN 978-1-78952-188-7

The right of Ben L. Connor to be identified
as the author of this work has been asserted by him
in accordance with the Copyright, Designs and Patents Act 1988.
All rights reserved. No part of this publication may be reproduced, stored in a
retrieval system or transmitted in any form or by any means, electronic, mechanical,
photocopying, recording or otherwise, without prior permission in writing from
Sonicbond Publishing Limited

Typeset in ITC Garamond & ITC Avant Garde
Printed and bound in England

Graphic design and typesetting: Full Moon Media

# on track ...
# Pearl
# Jam

every album, every song

Ben L. Connor

sonicbondpublishing.com

## Acknowlegements
This book is dedicated to my parents, who never stopped pushing me (in a good way!)

# on track ...

# Pearl Jam

## Contents

# Introduction

Why Pearl Jam?

If you're over 50 years old or under 30, chances are you are asking this question. Pearl Jam are one of the biggest-selling bands of their generation, with a devoted fan base and critical plaudits. They are one of the best live acts still active. They managed to survive the boom-and-bust of 1990s alt-rock while keeping their personal and musical integrity, and now fans and peers revere them as classic rock icons. And yet, for many, they remain artefacts of the *grunge* era: archetypal mopey Gen-X iconoclasts. If that's what you think, then this book is for you: to hopefully change your mind. If you're already a Pearl Jam fan, then this book is *also* for you! – to offer a new perspective on their music, and to shine a light on some of the hidden corners of their discography. Of course, you might disagree with my opinions on some songs, so feel free to disregard.

Their discography is so vast that I won't waste any more time on introductions. I will be going through their catalogue album by album, track by track. For every album that was re-released with bonus tracks, I will address those songs alongside the albums they're attached to. Every other non-album track, B-side and outtake, I will cover when they were released on compilations, so as to better convey the arc of Pearl Jam's career. Any leftovers will be covered at the end. I will not address every released alternate, live or demo version of each song in separate entries: with a couple of notable exceptions. Pearl Jam have not yet had a complete reissue campaign wherein every non-album track has been amended to the albums, which would enable record buyers to easily collect everything the band recorded. The order I've settled on should make clear where to find all the non-album tracks.

The story of Pearl Jam does not begin with their debut album, but with the bands the members came from, and the wider music scene around them. So, I will take some time to address the music of Green River, Mother Love Bone and Temple Of The Dog. I will give a track-by-track analysis of Temple Of The Dog's sole album, because it features the entirety of Pearl Jam's current lineup, and also because, it's just so good, it deserves the attention.

## Green River and Mother Love Bone

The roots of Pearl Jam go deep, and to understand the band, it's useful to know the context of the late-1980s Seattle music scene. Pearl Jam didn't burst forth overnight, fully formed from the brain of a marketing executive (as some accused them of being). The individual members had all paid their dues in other bands, and those bands are worth hearing for any Pearl Jam fan.

The founders of Pearl Jam – bassist Jeff Ament and guitarist Stone Gossard – got their start in the band Green River. They took that name from the song by Creedence Clearwater Revival: a band whose lack of pretension and dogged work ethic made them an acceptable influence to cite in the boomer-phobic post-punk era. The other members of Green River were vocalist/guitarist Mark Arm, guitarist Steve Turner, and drummer Alex Vincent.

Green River's first release was the *Come on Down* EP in 1985. After this, Turner left and was replaced by Bruce Fairweather. This lineup recorded another EP – *Dry As A Bone* (1987) – and the album *Rehab Doll* (1988) for the Seattle-based indie label Sub Pop, founded in 1986. The label heads Bruce Pavitt and Jonathan Poneman had a knack for spotting up-and-coming talents. They also released early records by iconic acts such as Nirvana, Soundgarden, Mark Lanegan, L7, The Afghan Whigs and Mudhoney – not to mention their spectacular undercard that included cult artists such as Tad, The Supersuckers, Love Battery, Scud Mountain Boys and Sunny Day Real Estate.

In Sub Pop promotional materials, Green River were described as 'ultra-loose GRUNGE that destroyed the morals of a generation'. Critic Everett True used that word 'grunge' to refer to the music of the Seattle scene, and it stuck, despite all involved hating it. According to Mark Yarm's book, *Everybody Love Our Town*, this is the origin of the term, that came to define an entire wave of rock music. 'Grunge' is an ugly word coined to describe some ugly music. Yet, like goth rock and air metal, it's a term that was once used derisively – and from which the bands so labelled, reflexively distanced themselves – but is now used fondly by fans and critics. The grunge era was short. It began with Nirvana's 1991 commercial breakthrough, and faded away after Kurt Cobain's suicide in 1994, but it was impactful. Grunge overturned traditional concepts of how rock music should sound and how rock stars should look and behave. A new marketing category – Alternative rock – emerged to incorporate all the strange and abrasive music – from funk metal to lo-fi – that was suddenly inexplicably popular. But before all that, there was Green River.

Green River's music is in the vein of The Stooges and MC5: atavistic garage rock with little nuance or sensitivity. That's a compliment by the way; there's a clarity of purpose to Green River's attack, that's admirable. Most of their songs consist of a single riff repeated relentlessly over punishingly hard 4/4 rhythms, with little room for the music to breathe. But their music isn't fast enough to be labelled punk, and there's a notable blues influence, which was supposedly *verboten* by post-punk purists.

The 1985 EP *Come on Down* is drenched in feedback and sounds primitive even by indie rock standards. The production is too thin to do justice to the playing's ferocity, and the vocals are mixed too low to really *sell* the songs. This EP includes the song 'Swallow My Pride', which is the closest thing Green River had to a hit. *Dry As a Bone* is much more forceful sonically, but the songs are still rudimentary. The best of this bunch is 'Unwind', on which the blues influence is most noticeable. *Rehab Doll* is their most fully-formed release. The sonic palette was expanded to include industrial-sounding percussion on 'Rehab Doll' and a rootsy acoustic intro for 'One More Stitch'. They also re-recorded 'Swallow My Pride', ditching the wah-wah guitar and including a coda lifted from Blue Oyster Cult's 'This Ain't The Summer Of Love'. The sprightly 'Together We'll Never' gets my vote for their best song, as it has a strong chorus hook.

Mark Arm's vocals are a most acquired taste. He doesn't sing, so much as cough up the words with the force of a full-body heave. In the vein of Iggy Pop circa The Stooges' *Fun House*, it feels like he's acting out the music's ferocity; the lyrics are of secondary importance to the aggressive feel. If you're hoping to catch a glimpse of the unique playing styles of Jeff Ament and Stone Gossard, you'll probably be disappointed. Ament's bass is frequently subsumed into the sonic murk, and Gossard's riffing – while expertly executed – didn't have the space to shine. It's no wonder these two players felt stifled by this band's self-imposed limitations.

Mark Arm was staunchly anti-careerist, and he viewed Ament and Gossard as attention-seeking stealth metalheads. They even wanted him to take singing lessons! In the late-1980s era of radio-polished glam metal, wanting to be an actual rock star was the worst accusation you could level at someone in the underground scene. In Michael Azerrad's chronicle of 1980s indie rock *Our Band Could Be Your Life*, Arm is quoted: 'There was a tension in the band for a while, and then it just got to be too great. It was punk rock versus a major-label deal'. When Ament invited label A&R men to a show, that was the final straw for Arm. The band broke up soon after recording *Rehab Doll*. Arm reunited with Steve Turner to form Mudhoney, who became grunge icons in their own right. A month after *Rehab Doll* was released, they dropped the first great grunge anthem: 'Touch Me, I'm Sick'.

The entire Green River discography, including non-album songs and demos, is available via expanded editions of their three releases. Somewhat surprisingly, Gossard and Ament would remain on good terms with their ex-bandmates. Green River reunited on stage during a Pearl Jam concert in Las Vegas on 30 November 1993. They also played a handful of headlining shows throughout 2008/2009.

Back in 1986, Green River had two non-album songs appear on the compilation *Deep Six*: released by another Seattle indie label C/Z Records. This compilation is often credited with planting the seed of the idea that there was a wider Seattle scene. The compilation tracklist also included future superstars Soundgarden, iconic cult heroes Melvins, and the underrated Skin Yard (whose guitarist was Jack Endino: the producer of *Dry as A Bone* and future releases by Soundgarden, Mudhoney and Nirvana). Another artist on the compilation was the goofily named Malfunkshun. This band dissolved not long after *Deep Six* was released, and its singer Andrew Wood began jamming with Jeff Ament and Stone Gossard. Eventually, Jeff Fairweather also joined, and with the edition of Gary Gilmore on drums, they became a band called Mother Love Bone. And this was the next step on the path to Pearl Jam.

Andrew Wood was a real character. Compared to his contemporaries in the Seattle scene, he was more openly influenced by 1970s glam and stadium rock. He was a lady-killing showman who wore makeup and flashy clothes and wandered out into the audience at shows. He developed a style of music he called 'love rock'. He also developed a drug problem, which persisted even after a stint in rehab in 1985.

Mother Love Bone could not have been more different from Green River, right down to their unfortunate double entendre moniker. Listening to their music with fresh ears, you'd find it hard to imagine that they and Mudhoney would ever be grouped together in the same scene. Mother Love Bone made unabashed cock rock in the vein of Aerosmith or Van Halen. While not nearly as good as those two bands (Who is?), they were more than a match for the sleazy over-produced likes of Mötley Crüe and Poison, who were tearing up the charts at the time. Mother Love Bone's music has a rough, warm, friendly feel. Gossard's riffs are simple and fast with rudimentary but effective chord changes. Wood's hippie-throwback lyrics about love children and star people, come across as guileless rather than pretentious.

In 1989, they released the four-song EP *Shine* on Mercury Records. The production is a little too flat to justify all the bluster, and the first three songs are largely forgettable, although 'Thru Fade Away' contains the line 'She's my hot ma-hot-ma Gandhi', which is either hilarious or appalling depending on your taste. The EP is essential though because the final song is 'Chloe Dancer/ Crown of Thorns' – the second truly great Seattle grunge song, and one of the finest that any Pearl Jam member has played on. It opens with a swirling piano figure played by Wood, that establishes a melancholy mood. Wood sings with surprising sensitivity about an ex-girlfriend who aspired to be a stripper. After two minutes, a chiming guitar riff kicks off the second part of the song, in which we also hear Jeff Ament's fretless bass for the first time. The song builds to a cathartic climax as Wood sings of how his drug problems destroyed his relationship. The line 'Dreams like this must die', would prove to be sadly prophetic.

The band re-recorded 'Crown of Thorns' – without the 'Chloe Dancer' introductory section – for their sole full-length album *Apple*, released in 1990. While not an out-and-out classic, *Apple* deserves a place on any discerning hard rock fan's shelf. It's comparable to Aerosmith's debut – under-produced and mostly one-note, but with obvious seeds of greatness. It's certainly the most *fun* album to come out of the Seattle grunge scene. Top songs include the strutting 'Stardog Champion' with a children's choir singing the refrain; 'Holy Roller', on which Wood delivers a spoken-word sermon about 'love rock', and the laid-back piano-led 'Gentle Groove'. But *Apple* suffers from the same self-imposed problem that plagued many albums at the turn of the decade: it's too long. By 1990, compact discs had become the default format, and many artists – including older rockers who should've known better – seemed to think that they needed to fill up the entire 75 minutes of available space, so they stopped judiciously trimming their albums down to the very best songs. *Apple* would be a stronger album at 40 minutes, as opposed to nearly an hour. That said, the best-value way to own this album is in the 1992 compilation that combined *Apple* and *Shine* onto one disc, with a bonus disc of two outtakes.

You can tell that Mother Love Bone's music would've really come into its own in a live setting. With a solid album to tour behind, it's likely they would've grown beyond their cult audience. One can imagine a parallel universe in which they played alongside other underground hard rock bands from the era, such as Jane's Addiction, Living Colour, King's X, and Warrior Soul. The combined force of these bands might've led to a different kind of alternative rock boom: one more influenced by Bowie than Iggy. But it was not to be. Andrew Wood died of a heroin overdose on 19 March 1990, just before *Apple* was released. That was a massive blow, not just because it scuppered Mother Love Bone's shot at success, but because Wood was well-loved by his bandmates. That love was evident in a project that was the next step on the path to Pearl Jam.

# Temple Of The Dog (1991)

Personnel:
Jeff Ament: bass,
Matt Cameron: drums, percussion
Chris Cornell: lead vocals, harmonica, banjo
Stone Gossard: rhythm guitar
Mike McCready: lead guitars
Eddie Vedder: backing vocals, co-lead vocals on 'Hunger Strike'
With:
Rick Parashar: piano, organ
Producer: Rick Parashar
Recorded at London Bridge Studio, Seattle, Washington, November/December 1990
Release date: 16 April 1991
Chart places: US: 5
Running time: 54:59

One person left devastated by Andrew Wood's death, was his former roommate Chris Cornell. Cornell was the singer and guitarist for Soundgarden, who at that time were probably the most well-established Seattle band. Their excellent 1989 album *Louder Than Love* was the first grunge album released on a major label, although it wasn't marketed as such; Soundgarden were seen at the time as guiding lights of the alternative metal scene, alongside Faith No More and Melvins.

Cornell learned of Wood's death, in-between tours, and while on the road, he wrote some songs in tribute to Wood. Upon returning to Seattle, Cornell approached Wood's ex-bandmates Gossard and Ament, to help record the songs. He brought along Soundgarden drummer Matt Cameron, and they were joined by two others: guitarist Mike McCready, and a surfer kid from San Diego called Eddie Vedder. Gossard, Ament, McCready and Vedder were in the process of forming the band that became Pearl Jam. This recording helped them solidify their musical chemistry.

The project took its name from Wood's lyrics for the Mother Love Bone song 'Man of Golden Words'. The original plan was to release Cornell's two songs – 'Say Hello 2 Heaven' and 'Reach Down' – as a single. But as they began to work on other pieces that Cornell, Gossard and Ament had prepared, it became clear that they had an album's worth of material. The album was recorded in only 15 days, and it was produced, engineered and mixed by one man: Rick Parashar, who also played piano and organ. The result is an example of the way great art can result from spontaneity and abandon. It's also a testament to rock-and-roll camaraderie; a genuine labour of love.

This music was very different from what Soundgarden were known for at the time, which was thick sludgy metal with odd time signatures. In comparison, Temple of The Dog were something of a classic-rock throwback: clear and bright, with strong melodies, but also with room for the players to stretch out. Cornell's soaring vocals have all the majesty of Robert Plant without any of the cock rock baggage. Despite being one of the catalysts for the grunge movement, this album sounds utterly timeless. If you were a radio DJ, you could play a song from this album between Faces and Bad Company, and your listeners wouldn't bat an eye.

The album was released on 16 April 1991, initially selling around 70,000 copies. That's a substantial number for a one-off spin-off project by the singer of an alternative metal band, made as a tribute to a man most of the public hadn't heard of – and that was before the record label A&M went all out promoting it. Initially, they were reluctant to market the album as involving the up-and-coming band newly dubbed Pearl Jam. But a year later, both Pearl Jam and Soundgarden were megastars, and A&M – to which neither band were signed – gave the album another push by releasing 'Hunger Strike' as a single. The album and single both charted on the US charts and the album went platinum by the end of 1992.

In 2016, for the album's 25th anniversary, its place in the classic-rock firmament was enshrined by the modern symbol of lasting success: the *super deluxe* multidisc re-release. This included demos, outtakes, live performances and a surround-sound mix. None of this is essential, but it grants insight into the band's development. Listening to this material, you can hear a great band coming together in real-time.

Temple Of The Dog played a few live shows throughout 1990-1992, and on a few occasions beyond that, Cornell joined Pearl Jam on stage to sing songs from the album. For the 25th anniversary, the band reunited for a short tour, where they played almost the entire album, plus covers of songs by acts as diverse as David Bowie, Harry Nilsson and The Cure, as well as a handful of Mother Love Bone songs. So, in a way, Andrew Wood managed to live out his rock star fantasies through the love and hard work of his friends.

## 'Say Hello 2 Heaven' (Cornell)

This is the first song that Cornell wrote in tribute to Wood, and we should all be so lucky as to have such a song written for us. Despite the Prince-like use of a number in the title, this is anything but a frivolous pop tune: it's an achingly sincere ballad on which every element comes straight from the heart. It's immediately apparent how well the players gelled. Every instrumentalist is given room to shine, but they all serve the song.

It opens with a gently descending three-note riff that settles into a gentle groove with comforting backing vocals. It sounds like how it feels to be drawn into a warm embrace. We get the first hints of the fluttery delicate-yet-tough guitar-playing – in the style of Hendrix's 'Little Wing' – that McCready would use to powerful effect on the Pearl Jam epics 'Black' and 'Yellow Ledbetter'.

Cornell's lyric paints a picture of Wood as a lost lamb: an innocent undone by forces he didn't understand. It's a lovely sentiment: to remember Wood as

15

his friends know him, and not as another victim of drugs. Of course, Wood was only the *first* grunge star to lose his life to drugs. There was darkness to come.

## 'Reach Down' (Cornell)

This is the second song Cornell wrote for Wood, and it's the album's big epic. In fact, at over 11 minutes, it's the longest song that Cornell or any of the Pearl Jam members have been involved in. Conventional wisdom would schedule it near the end of the album as the big emotional climax à la 'Layla' or 'Voodoo Chile'. But putting it near the start, helps establish that this is an album in which to immerse yourself.

The song opens with a growling riff that's packed with portent, and when the band slam in, it feels at first like this will be an angry song. But Cornell's lyrics are uplifting. He sings of Wood's desire to 'Reach down and lift the crowd up'. To Wood, and Cornell, being a rock singer is about more than posturing and preening and hogging the limelight: it's about elevating your audience; about inviting them into a shared experience. This is a generous vision of what it means to be a rock star: far away from the cynicism of other songs on the topic, such as Bowie's 'Ziggy Stardust'.

After four and a half minutes, the guitarists cut loose and solo for the rest of the song. It's not exactly up there with, say, Clapton and Allman's duel on 'Layla', but it has the same emotional weight; they aren't just showing off how good they are (although they are very very good). Rather, they are living out Wood's message of wild abandon. The moment at 8:45 when the music drops out and Cornell wails the chorus *a cappella* – harmonising with himself in the background – is one of the record's most powerful moments.

## 'Hunger Strike' (Cornell)

Enter one Mr. Edward Louis Severson III aka Eddie Vedder. This was his first-recorded lead vocal, and he makes a meal of it. He and Cornell sing a verse each and share the chorus. The song climaxes with them trading lines: Cornell's strangled wail contrasting with Vedder's sonorous tones. Vedder couldn't have asked for a better way to introduce himself to the public, except of course that most people would only hear this song after Pearl Jam broke through. This was released as a single in 1992 to re-promote the album, and the label highlighted the Pearl Jam connection, which embarrassed the band. Although, if they didn't want the publicity, they probably shouldn't have shot a video back in 1991. This became a fixture on MTV.

This is one of the most crowd-pleasing sing-along songs either Cornell or Pearl Jam have ever made. Pearl Jam's big anthems of the 1990s – like 'Alive' and 'Better Man' – had an undercurrent of darkness to them; Cornell's greatest songs with Soundgarden – like 'Hands All Over' and 'Black Hole Sun' – were rooted in bleak metaphors. 'Hunger Strike' is a clear-cut call for class consciousness. In the grand tradition of John Lennon's 'Working Class Hero', The Jam's 'The Eton Rifles' and Billy Bragg's entire discography, this is a song about class disparity: 'I don't mind stealing bread from the mouths of decadence/But I won't feed on the powerless when my cup's already overfilled'. This is hardly a radical political stance, and one has to acknowledge that there is always something a little cringeworthy in wealthy rock stars singing about the plight of the poor: just ask Bono. That said, these men were all struggling artists when they recorded this song, and it helped to enshrine Pearl Jam's blue-collar credentials.

When Cornell managed to join Pearl Jam on stage, this was inevitably the song he and Vedder chose to sing together. While it would be foolish to say that the song is timeless, it retains a naive charm that you won't find in other socially conscious 1990s songs, such as The Cranberries' 'Zombie' or 4 Non Blondes' 'What's Up'.

### 'Pushin' Forward Back' (Ament, Cornell, Gossard)
This is the album's first rocker, and it feels heavier than it is, compared to the songs surrounding it. The key ingredient is Matt Cameron. One of Soundgarden's unique qualities compared to their peers, was their use of unusual time signatures. While Cameron is hardly Bill Bruford, he gave songs such as 'Outshined' and 'My Wave' their extra kick by taking them beyond the basic 4/4 stomp that any other band would've played them as. When he joined Pearl Jam full-time, he brought that style to the band, and you can hear a preview of it on this song. It feels like the riff needs an extra beat to really land, so it's as if the song is rushing by slightly faster than you can follow. Vedder sings backing vocals here, but he's largely buried by the furious riffing and Cornell's full-throated roar. The lyric consists mainly of the pair shouting the title back and forth at each other. The phrase is a paradox that refers to how children push back against the mothers that nurture them.

### 'Call Me A Dog' (Cornell)
This is a song of relationship woes. It's an example of a common grunge trope where the singer puts words in someone else's mouth. Sonically and structurally, it's a cousin to 'Say Hello 2 Heaven'. The slow swinging rhythm creates a bluesy late-night atmosphere, and there is some nice concise lead guitar fills from McCready. For a lesser album track, its sense of drama and dynamics surpasses most of Green River or Mother Love Bone's music.

### 'Times Of Trouble' (Cornell, Gossard)
This is a song of support for someone going through hard times, and it's the album's hidden gem. It builds from a comforting opening to a triumphant climax, without seeming pompous. With its combination of electric and acoustic sounds – including lovely piano played by Parashar, and judicious harmonica played by Cornell – this song is cut from the same cloth as 1960s/1970s singer-songwriter classics such as Tim Hardin's 'Reason To Believe', Jackson Browne's 'Late For The Sky' and Elton John's 'Madman Across The Water'.

On the verses, Cornell sings in a steady and reassuring manner, and on the chorus, he really belts it out, leaving the listener in no doubt that – as the theme from *Friends* put it – he'll be there for you. This may be the most straightforward lyric Cornell ever penned. There are references to needles and spoons: the tools of a heroin user. It's as if Cornell is offering Wood the support he wished he could've given while his friend was alive: 'Hold on to your time till you break through these times of trouble'. He almost whispers the final word of the chorus. It's as if he knew there were worse troubles to come for him and his friends in the Seattle scene.

The song's music has a storied history. Gossard brought the opening guitar figure to this project, but it was also included on the demo Jack Irons gave to Eddie Vedder. Vedder added his own lyrics, and that version was developed into the Pearl Jam B-side 'Footsteps' (see *Lost Dogs*). That song is great, but this is exceptional.

### 'Wooden Jesus' (Cornell)
This song opens with a Matt Cameron specialty: an off-kilter drum rhythm that's part-way between funk and math rock. Wood block adds to the exotic feel. The track swings along nicely without catching fire, but it's a solid addition to the album, if only as an opportunity for Cameron to shine. Cornell's lyric addresses the title object: a tacky piece of mass-produced religious symbolism. Cornell treats the icon as the embodiment of the commercialisation of religion. 'Where are you from?/Korea, Canada, or maybe Taiwan?'. In other words, this supposedly sacred symbol is just another cheaply made consumer item. 'Can I be saved?/I spent all my money on a future grave'. Are people forsaking spiritual salvation by focusing instead on consumption? Songs criticising organised religion were a dime-a-dozen in the 1980s and 1990s, but at least this one has a specific point of view and isn't just religion-bad.

### 'Your Saviour' (Cornell)
Another catchy Cameron drum rhythm for another song that's cynical towards religion. This one addresses the issue through the prism of a relationship. Cornell could be singing from the perspective of a Messiah figure who is questioning whether he is what his followers really need. Or Cornell could be casting himself as the wronged party in a failing relationship (something he had done before on Soundgarden's 'Jesus Christ Pose'). This is not especially different from the preceding song, except for Gossard getting funky on the guitar, and lashings of wah-wah from McCready.

### 'Four Walled Room' (Cornell, Gossard)
This is the least-good song on the album. It opens with an exotic guitar figure reminiscent of The Doors' 'The End'. The Doors were one of the most obvious but least openly acknowledged influences on 1990s alt-rock. This was partly

due to the cult of Jim Morrison the rock poet martyr, that peaked with Oliver Stone's 1990 film biopic. It just wasn't *cool* anymore to act as if your lyrics had any deep psychological and mythological significance. This song could've used a dose of Jim Morrison's energy though because it's mostly an overly long dirge that builds slowly to its wailing finale. The song is about feeling trapped by one's own thoughts, and – fittingly, as the title is repeated over and over – it does seem as if the walls are closing in on the listener. Vedder sings backup on this, but his vocals are largely buried under the squall.

## 'All Night Thing' (Cornell)
This song is the perfect closer, in that it's a simple pleasant tune that, after some weightier tracks, reconnects with the listener on a personal level. Its jazzy after-hours vibe makes it feel as if the curtains are being drawn and things are winding down for the evening. Cameron's drums swing, while the guitars take a back seat to organ and piano: played by Parashar (the album's unsung hero). Musically, this isn't far off from the music Van Morrison was making around the same time: such as 'Have I Told You Lately That I Love You?'. With *him* singing, this could've easily become a dinner party background staple.

As Cornell relays the story of a one-night stand, his vocal is perfectly judged: charming and seductive without being sleazy. After this album, he and Cameron returned to Soundgarden to make two of the greatest rock albums of the decade, and one other pretty good album. It's notable that after this project, Cornell's personality came to dominate Soundgarden's music more with each album, for better *and* for worse.

The remaining members of Temple of The Dog stayed together and decided to make a go of it with this Vedder kid. So, let's see how that turned out.

# Ten (1991)

Personnel:

Jeff Ament: bass

Stone Gossard: rhythm guitar, backing vocals

Dave Krusen: drums, timpani

Mike McCready: lead guitar

Eddie Vedder: vocals

With:

Rick Parashar: piano, organ, percussion

Walter Gray: cello

Producer: Rick Parashar

Recorded at London Bridge Studio, Seattle, Washington, March-April 1991

Release date: 27 August 1991

Chart places: US: 2, UK: 18

Running time: 53:20

Most great bands have a memorable origin story: Keith Richards noticing that Mick Jagger was carrying a Muddy Waters record; John Lydon spotted wearing a homemade 'I hate Pink Floyd' shirt; Jack White pretending that he and his ex-wife were siblings. Pearl Jam's origin story quickly became a key part of their mythos, even more so because it was shrouded in controversy and misinformation.

After Wood's death, Gossard sent a cassette of demos he had worked up to his friend Jack Irons down in Los Angeles. Irons had been the drummer in Red Hot Chili Peppers before they broke through in 1989. Irons passed that cassette to a visitor from San Diego: Eddie Vedder. Vedder met with Gossard and Ament, and then after listening to the demos, he went surfing. While out on the ocean, lyrics for those songs came to him. 'I was literally writing some of these words as I was going up against a wave', band biographer Kim Neely quoted him as saying in 1991.

There's an element of romance to this story. Surfing is often talked about in spiritual terms, as a way to free your mind and tune in to nature. So, the idea that these songs came to Vedder like a bolt out of the blue makes it seem as if it was fate itself that lead him to Pearl Jam. To fans, this story made it seem that Pearl Jam were not just another rock band. To be taken seriously – especially in holier-than-thou punk rock circles – bands must avoid the idea that they were in any way contrived by the music industry; they need to have come into being, organically, driven only by the need to express themselves artistically. This is mostly all nonsense of course: even The Beatles and The Stones were originally marketed the same way bands are today. But a strong core mythology can help a band survive the inevitable backlash and cries of sellout. And so, it was with Pearl Jam.

Vedder sent the band a tape of him singing his lyrics. This became known as the *Momma-Son* demo, after the lyrical narrative connecting the songs. The band immediately saw potential. According to Neely, Ament told Gossard, 'I may be totally whacked-out, but I think this guy is amazing'. They brought Vedder up to try things out, and within a week they knew it would work. Vedder described it to Neely as 'the most intense musical experience I'd ever been involved in', and Ament said, 'That week was one of the greatest weeks of my life'.

They dubbed their new band Mookie Blaylock, after their favourite basketball player. It's hard to imagine a band with that name selling millions of records, and they changed it when they signed to a label. But it's not as if 'Pearl Jam' is an especially great name either. The band's moniker has its own mysterious origin story. The most obvious explanation – and the one that was repeated in the schoolyard by snickering boys – was that 'pearl jam' was slang for sperm. The band have denied this and insisted that the name comes from Vedder's great-grandmother's homemade peyote jam. But that explanation has never been particularly convincing, and now, most people just brush past the name and focus on the music.

The band got to work turning the demos into proper songs. Gossard and Ament brought in more ideas they had leftover from Mother Love Bone, and McCready added his input. In the end, the music for most of the songs was credited to Gossard and/or Ament, while Vedder was credited for all lyrics. The fifth band member at this time was Dave Krusen, on drums. Krusen is the Pete Best of the Pearl Jam story, except that he actually got to record with the band and reap some of the rewards. But this was his only album with them. While not the most technically accomplished or distinctive drummer, his style suited these songs perfectly. In an era when hard rock drums were so close-mic'ed and electronically processed that they might as well have been drum machines, Krusen's drumming was loose and limber, and sounded like an organic part of the music

Determined to honour Blaylock in some way, the album title comes from his jersey number. The cover isn't particularly inventive, but it is effective for two reasons. The main cover is just the hands with the band's name behind them. But if you unfold the CD booklet, you see the band standing facing each other, touching hands: a potent symbol of camaraderie. The other memorable thing about the cover is the backdrop's lurid purple colour, which is distinctive and eye-catching. The lyrics inside the cover are handwritten and incomplete, as they are for most Pearl Jam albums. This creates a sense of personal connection and encourages fans to interpret the songs for themselves.

The band signed to Epic Records: a subsidiary first of CBS and then Sony. This raised eyebrows, although they were far from the first (or even the hundredth) alternative band to sign with a major label. Many before them had crashed and burned, and Pearl Jam were far from being considered most likely to succeed. *Ten* was released on 27 August 1991: a full month before Nirvana's 'Smells Like Teen Spirit' started its slow crawl up the charts and turned all eyes and ears towards Seattle. And Nirvana were not the only competition the band faced.

1991 is arguably one of the most significant years in rock history. To the Generation X, August-September of that year is comparable to 1967's Summer of Love, in terms of the quantity of earthshaking music released. On 12 August, Metallica released their self-titled 'Black Album', which introduced angry, scary, genuinely *heavy* metal to the mainstream. 3 September saw the release of Primal Scream's dance/rock hybrid *Screamadelica*: the last great artistic statement from the Madchester indie rock scene, and an essential step in the mainstreaming of electronic dance music. On 17 September, Guns N' Roses finally followed up their iconic debut *Appetite For Destruction* with the monumental *Use Your Illusion* twin albums. A 'White Album' for the 1990s, this was two and a half hours of over-written, overproduced, over-the-top rock that left nothing for other hair metal bands to accomplish. In fact, it was such a 'Follow that!' moment, that Guns N' Roses themselves fell apart before *they* could even try.

Pull back a bit, and 1991 contains even more riches. On 12 March, R.E.M.'s *Out of Time* and its single 'Losing My Religion' turned *those* college rock oddballs into unlikely superstars. On 28 May, Smashing Pumpkins' debut *Gish* laid the foundations for their future success. On 18 July, Perry Farrell of Jane's Addiction launched the first Lollapalooza tour, which became the Monterey Pop of the alt-rock era. On 4 November, My Bloody Valentine released *Loveless* – the album that defined the shoegaze scene. On 18 November, the perennially-uncool U2 managed to successfully reinvent themselves as art rock pranksters with *Achtung Baby*. Beyond that, there's also Teenage Fanclub's Britpop template *Bandwagonesque*, Matthew Sweet's update of 1970s power pop *Girlfriend*, Crowded House's gorgeous *Woodface*, cult weirdos Primus' *Sailing The Seas Of Cheese*, Stevie Ray Vaughan's posthumous collection *The Sky Is Crying*, the final good albums by Ozzy Osbourne (*No More* Tears) and Van Halen (*For Unlawful Carnal Knowledge*), the chart-topping Garth Brooks album *Ropin' The Wind* which saw country music fully cross over into the pop arena, and – lest we forget – Enya's greatest album *Shepherd Moons*.

And that was only *some* of the competition that Pearl Jam was up against. One day alone – 24 September 1991 – saw the release of three era-defining classics: Soundgarden's *Badmotorfinger*, Red Hot Chili Peppers' *Blood Sugar Sex Magick*, and Nirvana's *Nevermind*. That last album is now enshrined in the mass consciousness as *the* great grunge album, and *the* album that turned the music industry on its head. But it's important to remember that in that last regard, it had plenty of help from all those other epochal releases.

*Ten* slowly ascended up the *Billboard* chart to peak at number 2 in May 1992: nine months after its release. To continuously accumulate sales and airplay over such a long period, amidst such competition for people's eardrums, is evidence that Pearl Jam's rise was a grassroots phenomenon, earned via hard work and talent.

*Ten* is now generally regarded, if not as having the same totemic status as *Nevermind*, to be just as good and just as important an album. In Colin

Larkin's massive 1998 *All-Time Top 1000 Albums* poll of fans and critics, it was ranked at 83, between Jeff Buckley's *Grace* and Nirvana's *In Utero*; good company indeed. When *Rolling Stone* magazine conducted a poll of artists and critics for their *500 Greatest Albums Of All Time* feature in 2003, *Ten* was ranked at 207. In the new 2020 poll, it was moved up to 160: a surprise given that poll's avowedly anti-rockist mandate. It was still ranked below Taylor Swift and Drake, so take that with a grain of salt. In comparison, the determinedly rock-loving readers of *Classic Rock* magazine voted it 35th in their *100 Greatest Rock Albums Of All Time* poll. That was the highest position for a band that debuted in the 1990s, and one place above *Nevermind*. My point is that the album has stood the test of time, even as it remains inexorably tied to its era.

Some international editions of *Ten* included bonus tracks. Bonus tracks were introduced in the CD era, to the irritation of hardcore fans who need to buy every edition to get the exclusive tracks. This is the only Pearl Jam album that suffered from that practice. The European edition included a live version of 'Alive', and the B-sides 'Wash' and 'Dirty Frank' which I will discuss in the entry for *Lost Dogs*. The Japanese edition included an isolated track of 'Master/Slave', and a cover of The Beatles' 'I've Got A Feeling', which I'll discuss in the Extras section. In 2009, *Ten* was reissued in a massive collector's edition, which I will discuss as a separate entry after this.

## 'Once' (Gossard, Vedder)

Album one, track one is the moment for a band to make a statement about who they are and what they stand for. The opening song on a debut album can be how new listeners first encounter a band. These opening tracks can become a band's signature song and genre-or-era-defining anthems in their own right. Think of Black Sabbath's self-titled song from the self-titled album, which more-or-less invented heavy metal; think the Ramones' 'Blitzkrieg Bop': the ultimate punk party-starter and go-to needle drop for unimaginative filmmakers who need to signify youthful exuberance; think Guns N' Roses' 'Welcome To The Jungle': a song that mythologized the band, their city and their scene, by giving hard rock a new dose of street cred. 'Once' is not among this number. It *is* a great song – easily the equal of, say, the *second* songs on the debut albums by Black Sabbath, Ramones or Guns N' Roses. It's definitely one of the top five Pearl Jam opening songs. It has a great sense of dynamics, as each musical element is introduced with a dramatic flourish, and Gossard's central riff rises and falls, sweeping the listener along. But in comparison to the rest of *Ten,* it's not particularly great.

What it is though, is one of the greatest-ever introductions to a vocalist. After a soft, slinky, curtain-raising instrumental piece with exotic percussion that makes it sound as if you're being welcomed into the band's inner sanctum, a wild riff emerges from out of the smoke, and then Vedder enters with a roar: 'IIIIIIIIIIII admit it! What's to say?'. It's hard to think of another singer who introduced themselves with as much power and presence in their very first note (discounting 'Hunger Strike', since that didn't reach the wider public until after *Ten*'s success). Right from the off, Vedder is singing in first person, talking directly to the audience. That opening line, frames this song as a confession from him to us. That is an effective way to get the listener invested. However, this is not actually Eddie Vedder singing these words: he is singing in character. His use of this lyric technique on *Ten* and the next few albums, distinguished him from his peers in the grunge scene – especially Kurt Cobain, whose unflattering soul-bearing lyrics helped establish the idea that all grunge music was self-absorbed navel-gazing. It would become difficult to tell without context whether Vedder was singing in character or as himself. But this song is clear-cut.

'Once' began as one of the Gossard demos that Vedder listened to in Los Angeles (as did 'Alive' and 'Footsteps'). Vedder came up with lyrics to those three songs together, and they form a narrative trilogy of which 'Once' is, confusingly, the middle segment. Knowing this *Momma-Son* story – or even knowing there *was* a story connecting these three songs – was something that distinguished hardcore Pearl Jam fans from the casuals. The story is this: 'Alive' is sung from the perspective of an abused young boy; 'Once' tells of him unleashing his pent-up rage; 'Footsteps' is him looking back at how he ended up (in jail, presumably). It's a tragic tale that appealed to hard rock fans with a sensitive side. In 'Once', the protagonist is stuck reliving his abusive childhood in his mind. Once upon a time, he could forget that – he could lose himself – thanks to his relationship with a special someone. But now that relationship is over, and he can't control himself anymore.

The genius of this song is that it works even if you don't know the story. Vedder sings the verses almost too fast to follow, but the chorus is high melodrama: 'Once/Upon a time/I could control myself'. To the casual radio listener primed by hair metal, that line could read as typical cock-rock horniness. To alternative rock fans, that line could be directed at society in general, as if to say, 'I ain't gonna let The Man control me'. Either way, it's the kind of song that could get any listener on board.

## 'Even Flow' (Gossard, Vedder)

Every great band has a quintessential song that's not their absolute best but is the song that defines the essence of their sound; their chemistry; their *modus operandi*. It's usually a fist-pumping anthem with a dash of self-mythologising: such as The Rolling Stones' 'Jumpin' Jack Flash', Led Zeppelin's 'Whole Lotta Love', The Clash's 'Complete Control' and U2's 'Pride (In the Name Of Love)'. If I had to pick one for Pearl Jam, this song is a good candidate.

It opens with a fantastic upwards-reaching riff that snaps you to attention. After this furious flourish, everything pauses for the guitars to gather steam again, and Vedder enters with another long-sustained howl. Critics quickly latched onto his tendency to run words together, as a defining feature of the band. Evidence for that was Adam Sandler's spoof of this song on the 9 October 1993 episode of *Saturday Night Live*. It didn't do the song any harm.

Plenty of bands have found success with unintelligible lyrics (Heck, R.E.M. built their career on it!). In fact, in the years before you could look them up on the internet, indecipherable lyrics gave a band some extra mystique. Consider how it was a selling point of Nirvana's 'Lithium' single that it had the lyrics for *Nevermind* printed inside the cover.

In this case, the chorus is strong enough to make understanding irrelevant, even if the only words most people heard were 'Even flow'. It's the following lyrics that show the depths of Vedder's songwriting: 'Thoughts arrive like butterflies/He don't know, and so he chases them away'. It's a song about mental illness and how that results in homelessness: as made clear by the line, 'Rests his head on a pillow made of concrete'. The liner notes do not include the complete lyrics, just the chorus written around a US dollar bill: clearly making a statement about the plight of the dispossessed in the richest country on earth. In contrast to 'Once', Vedder is singing in the third person here, acting as a righteously indignant observer of society's ills.

This was released in April 1992 as the band's second single, seven months after the album was released. *Ten* had sold slowly but steadily until the label correctly surmised that with this extra push, it could blow up. The song was a rock-radio hit, but it was only available as a physical single outside the US, and so it became a hot import item; doubly so because the single version was a different recording of the song (see *Rearviewmirror*).

## 'Alive' (Gossard, Vedder)

What do Pearl Jam have in common with Eagles, Sex Pistols, Phil Collins, Boston and Kate Bush? It's that their debut single might be their best song. For people of a certain age, 'Alive' is as iconic as 'Take It Easy' or 'Anarchy In The U.K.', and just like those songs it captures a particular time and place and cultural mood. It immediately became an alternative radio staple, and I suspect that over-familiarity has lead some to dismiss it. But it remains one of Pearl Jam's – and grunge rock's – most iconic anthems.

Its structure – building from slow mournful verses to a lengthy guitar solo – gives it a cathartic power similar to Lynyrd Skynyrd's 'Free Bird' and Pink Floyd's 'Comfortably Numb'. It deserves those comparisons. From the fanfare-like opening riff to the soaring chorus to the climactic solo, every part of this song seems designed for maximum impact. But its success is due to more than those basic building blocks – the contrast between Vedder's larger-than-life chorus and his conversational singing style on the verses, made the song an object of fascination. This was hard rock music that made you *think* as well as feel. At least you'd hope so. But you can never underestimate the public's capacity to focus on the surface pleasures of a song and ignore its deeper meaning. Think The Police' 'Every Breath You Take'; think Bruce Springsteen's 'Born in The U.S.A.'; think of the chorus of Nirvana's 'In Bloom', released a month after this: 'He's the one who likes all our pretty songs/And he likes to sing along ... But he knows not what it means'.

So what does 'Alive' mean? Well, it started life as a demo called 'Dollar Short' that was on the tape Gossard sent Vedder, and Vedder's lyric turned into the first instalment of the trilogy that also comprises 'Once' and 'Footsteps'. These songs were nicknamed the *Momma-Son* trilogy, based largely on the lyrics of this song. The first verse tells the story plainly:

'Son', she said, 'Have I got a little story for you
What you thought was your daddy was nothing but a...
While you were sitting home alone at age 13
Your real daddy was dying'

It's a family drama straight out of a southern gothic novel – a boy lied to by his mother, not knowing who his real father was until it's too late. The second verse is even darker but more open to interpretation:

Oh, she walks slow across a young man's room
She says, 'I'm ready for you'
I can't remember anything till this very day
Except love

Whether he's singing about sexual abuse or not, it's clear that whatever he can't remember, left a deep emotional scar. It's a dark story, and of course people wondered if it was autobiographical. Vedder *did* learn that the man he thought was his biological father, was not, but the rest of the song is fiction. Not that that stopped the speculation. It's easy to ignore all the context when the music is so galvanising.

While this song is not an albatross around the band's neck in the way that, say, 'Creep' is for Radiohead, there is a bit of cognitive dissonance regarding the song's success. With a chorus as perfectly simple as 'I'm still alive!', you can't exactly fault the audience for getting amped-up by it. But Vedder meant that as an expression of survivor's guilt: 'My father's dead and yet I'm still alive'. It's a tragic tale, yet today it is blasted on the radio five times a day in between Bon Jovi's 'Livin' on A Prayer' and Van Halen's 'Hot For Teacher' like it's any old jock jam. But the fans know better. 'Alive' is an example of how people can take a work of art, and reinterpret it to make it more meaningful for them. Rather than ignoring the song's dark undercurrents, the fans have reframed it as a story about overcoming personal tragedy. The chorus is now a cry of resilience, and it makes for one of the most cathartic communal comments of any Pearl Jam concert. The image on the single's cover – Ament's stick-figure drawing of a man reaching up with both hands as if in praise (now known as Stickman) – has become the most common image associated with Pearl Jam, and a common choice of tattoo for fans of the band.

Like 'Even Flow', the 'Alive' single was only available physically in the USA as an import single, so it never charted on the *Billboard* Hot 100. It was a huge hit on every rock airplay chart though. It reached 16 in the UK and 9 in Australia. Australia is particularly fond of the song – in 1998, the radio station Triple J (who run the world's biggest annual music poll) ran their Hottest 100 Of All Time poll, and 'Alive' came in third, behind Hunters & Collectors' 'Throw Your Arms Around Me' (which Pearl Jam would cover live) and, of course, Nirvana's 'Smells Like Teen Spirit'. *Classic Rock* readers also voted it as one of the 100 greatest rock songs ever, and it managed to survive *Rolling Stone*'s 2021 rock canon overall to be included in their list of the 500 greatest songs. For once, the fans *and* the critics both got it right.

## 'Why Go' (Ament, Vedder)

The album does not let up: this is the fourth hard-rocking song in a row. Vedder sings in third-person again, this time about a girl confined to a mental institution.

The drum pattern that kicks the song off, sounds like the girl beating at the walls of her cell, and Ament's thick bass line evokes a frantic heartbeat. It's all a bit over the top, especially when Vedder calls the doctor 'some stupid fuck'. But he really sells the lyric, with one of his most aggressive vocal performances ever.

## 'Black' (Gossard, Vedder)

This track cuts in before 'Why Go' has even faded away, as if the band can't wait for you to hear it. And for good reason: this is the song that – alongside 'Alive' – is commonly cited as Pearl Jam's finest. If 'Alive' is the public's choice, then 'Black' is the fans' choice. It's certainly their most iconic ballad. It's a song about letting go of a loved one; about the pain of admitting that a relationship isn't working. It's just as much a song of resilience as 'Alive' is, except that 'Black' is about facing up to your own failings. No wonder it resonates with people.

Vedder gives a career-defining performance, leavening his raw emotional outpouring with good taste. His voice is innately powerful, but he lets his vulnerability slip in the way he pauses between words on lines such as, 'All I taught her was… everything', or groans his way into the line 'Twisted thoughts that spin 'round my head'. When the song reaches its climax, he doesn't scream and repeat himself 'Baby baby baby'-style *à la* Robert Plant but roars out 'I know you'll be a beautiful star in someone's sky/But why can't it be mine?' and sounds like he's in genuine pain. It's not autobiographical, but it sounds as if it could be.

Musically, this is the *Ten* song that feels most like a carry-over from Temple of The Dog. It has a similar guileless, quasi-homemade feel, exemplified by the lo-fi introduction. It sounds distant like you're listening to the song on an old transistor radio, When Ament's fretless bass swoops in, it's as if the door is opened and the band is pulling you into their private huddle. Rick Parashar's piano and Hammond organ contributions are also essential in giving this song its earthy soulful feel: similar to 'Times of Trouble' but darker. Another crucial component is Gossard's rhythm guitar – rather than doubling down on the darkness with melodramatic power chords, he plays delicate fluttery chords that accentuate the melancholy. When – at the climax of the song – Vedder goes into a wordless refrain and the guitars blend in with the melody, it's a stirring moment.

Despite being arguably the greatest ballad of the entire grunge era, 'Black' is a genuinely timeless song. The basic bones of this song are so solid, that it would've been a hit if Bush, Candlebox or Silverchair had recorded it. But those bands and a dozen others, likely wouldn't have existed without Pearl Jam, and this song.

Famously, the band refused to release it as a single. They feared it would make them too popular, and it almost certainly would have. (It reached 3 on the rock radio chart, regardless.) This was an intensely personal song, and the band didn't fancy it being lumped in with the pompous power ballads of the era (like 'November Rain' and 'Bed Of Roses'). That might seem like the height of rock star arrogance – only in the early-1990s could rock bands actively try to resist success and not be met with eye rolls. But this was an example of choosing art over commerce. It paid off in the end, because – unlike those karaoke favourites – this song has retained its mystique. It still feels like you're listening in on Vedder's primal scream therapy.

## 'Jeremy' (Ament, Vedder)

Not content with unleashing 'Alive' and 'Black' in quick succession, Pearl Jam now released their third and most infamous stone-cold classic. It opens with a chiming guitar motif and a bass rumble and that sounds like storm clouds brewing. This riff is developed into a groove that runs through the whole song. This is undeniably the album's most *propulsive* song: it sweeps the listener up into an emotional maelstrom.

This song is another of Vedder's potted psychodramas. The Jeremy of the title is a bullied boy who snaps, with tragic results. The lyrics alternate between third and first-person, with Vedder switching from observer to narrator. Like Quint from *Jaws*, he starts to relive the tragedy as he relates it. The first verse paints a picture of a disturbed child with neglectful parents, who draws violent fantasies. In the second verse, Vedder inserts himself into the story: as one of the bullies who picked on the boy and drove him to violence. The ominous chorus 'Jeremy spoke in class today', begs the question: what did he say? The music video helped to clarify the matter somewhat. The 'Jeremy' clip – directed by Mark Pellington – is one of the defining pop artefacts of the grunge era. It won four MTV Video Music awards in 1993, including Best Video. More than most attention-grabbing music videos from this time (like for instance, Michael Jackson's self-conscious 'Black Or White' video, which had its own prime-time special), 'Jeremy' still has the power to shock and discomfort. It was instrumental in breaking Pearl Jam wide, and in making Eddie Vedder a star.

Vedder's appearance in the video is galvanising – lit in high contrast, he looks suitably intense and Byronic: the epitome of a brooding serious artist. When he sings some of the harsher lines, his face takes on an almost demonic appearance. His singing shots are intercut with a boy playing Jeremy who acts out the lyrics amidst a disquieting barrage of fire, strobe lights and biblical passages. It's the final sequence that's the most shocking – Jeremy enters a classroom, takes out a gun, and the camera cuts to the other students: frozen in shock with blood splattered over them. Many people interpreted this as meaning Jeremy had opened fire on his classmates, but the true meaning was that he died by suicide. The reason for the confusion is that the video's most widely shown version was censored so that the gun was barely visible, and it's hard to make out that Jeremy puts it in his own mouth. As tactless as it is to say, this controversy was one of the talking points that helped raise Pearl Jam's profile.

The story was a blend of two real-life cases – a boy Vedder knew in high school, who brought a gun to school but didn't kill himself, and a suicide that he read about in a newspaper. That got Vedder thinking about how some people think to use suicide as a form of revenge on their tormentors, and how futile that is. While this song is rooted in those specific tragedies, it, unfortunately, remains relevant today. The song has transcended its origins and is now seen as a statement on America's violent gun culture: as symbolised by the single's chilling cover art which showed a toddler reaching for a handgun. The video was re-released onto YouTube for National Gun Violence Awareness Day in 2020.

This song was another big hit on rock radio. But unlike 'Alive' or 'Even Flow', it's not a headbanging anthem. There's no sense of catharsis. The climax with Vedder howling wordlessly, is a cry of despair rather than a sing-along moment. This subject matter was not unprecedented (The Boomtown Rats had a hit with 'I Don't Like Mondays', which actually *was* about a mass shooting), but what was original about 'Jeremy' was the singer painting himself in such negative terms. Vedder owns up to the wrongs he did, not to a woman (this ain't a country song) but to an innocent boy. One couldn't imagine Garth Brooks admitting that he picked on a boy because he was a 'harmless little fuck'. This kind of confessional writing made it clear that Pearl Jam were not a band prone to self-glorification.

## 'Oceans' (Ament, Gossard, Vedder)

This is the album's shortest and softest song, and it works as an interlude between the era-defining attack of the first half and the relatively underappreciated second half. It opens with Vedder's voice distorted by a watery effect floating over gentle chords, and rumbling bass. The melody is negligible, and in lieu of a proper chorus, there's thundering timpani from Krusen. This is Pearl Jam's first impressionistic song. It evokes the feel of waves rising and falling as storm clouds brew. You'd think it was about a sailor lost at sea, but it's actually a love song inspired by Vedder's surfing. This was the first of many times he referenced that hobby in a Pearl Jam song.

'Oceans' was released as the fourth and final single from *Ten*, which is baffling, because there was no way this unassuming wisp of a song could be a hit, and it wasn't. The accompanying music video consists of black and white footage of the band performing and Vedder surfing in Hawaii. It's notable mainly because it was the last music video Pearl Jam would make for eight years.

## 'Porch' (Vedder)

Just when you thought the album was mellowing out, this song pumps up and bites your head off. Vedder's voice leaps out with the attention-grabbing line, 'What the fuck is this world coming to?', while Gossard lays down some of the most Green River-esque guitar on the album. After a few minutes of Vedder ranting about a failed relationship, the music slows down and opens up for McCready to deliver the album's best solo: yes, maybe even better than that on 'Alive'. This relatively unassuming and otherwise forgettable album track became the band's big live guitar jam showcase. In fact, it's their third-most-played song, after 'Even Flow' and 'Alive'. Performances of 'Porch' often stretch to ten minutes, and McCready uses every moment of that to justify his status as a guitar hero for the Generation X. His playing is less about showing his technique, and more about getting lost in the music.

## 'Garden' (Gossard, Vedder)

It is hard for an album this massively successful to have underrated deep cuts, but if such a thing exists on *Ten,* it's 'Garden'. The twinkling music-box-like guitar figure that opens it, sets a secretive midnight mood, perfect for Vedder's emotionally vulnerable lyrics. The garden of the title seems to refer to a secret place inside someone where they're disconnected from the world, and Vedder is determined to break in there. The sky scraping chorus is one of the album's best showcases for his sonorous voice. McCready's luscious bluesy solo is the cherry on top; the drawn-out note at the start of it is truly beautiful.

## 'Deep' (Gossard, Vedder)

This is probably the album's weakest track, and even then, it's not bad, just ordinary. The lyrics reference suicide and drug use, but they aren't particularly memorable. The music is distinguished mainly by the swing rhythm, and the excessive use of the wah-wah pedal. *Ten* is perfect as it is, but replacing 'Deep' with a finished version of 'Brother' would arguably have made it even more perfect. That said, the freaked-out squiggly ending is the perfect lead-in to the perfect closing track.

## 'Release' (Ament, Gossard, Krusen, McCready, Vedder)

Throughout their career, the one thing Pearl Jam have been reliably good at, is ending an album. Some bands try to climax with an all-stops-out epic, while others tuck their least interesting songs away at the end. Pearl Jam's album closers are always ballads, and they usually serve as a manifesto outlining the band's state of mind. And so it is with 'Release'. Vedder drops his characters, and sings a stirring song of self-affirmation. The song fades in on an uplifting circular guitar figure, and it builds in intensity as Vedder struggles against the unnamed forces holding him back. As the song nears its end, waves of guitars crash against him, and just when they threaten to overwhelm him, the song cuts out and fades away on some gentle chords.

While Vedder could not have known that this album would make him a superstar, that context adds an element of irony to lines like 'I'll ride the wave where it takes me'. Who is Vedder speaking to when he roars 'Release me'? Is it society? His family? Himself? It could be all of them or no one in particular. Like much of the best rock music – especially the kind that connects with people on a deep level and turns them into lifelong fans – it's open to interpretation. We all have things (bonds, obligations, relationships) that we long to be released from, and this song is a cry for freedom that touches that primal desire.

'Release' quickly became a fan favourite. Noted American critic Steven Hyden ranked it as Pearl Jam's number-one song. It is often (but not always) played in concert. When it *is* played, it's usually as the set opener, which inverts its meaning from an expression of longing into a declaration of intent. Pearl Jam quickly built a reputation as a great live band; each concert feels like they're releasing everything they have and holding nothing back.

## 'Master/Slave' (Ament, Vedder)

When I said 'Release' was the perfect closing track, that wasn't exactly true, for this is the inevitable hidden track. It seems that in the early-1990s, every alt-rock band had to include a hidden track. Sometimes these were complete songs, sometimes they were jams (such as Nirvana's 'Endless, Nameless' on *Nevermind*, which arguably popularised the idea), and sometimes they were scraps of ideas that the band included as a gift to listeners who played the album all the way through and didn't just skip to the singles. The latter would be the case for most Pearl Jam albums from this point forwards.

In this instance though, it's the full version of the instrumental that opened the album, and hearing the full version is a treat. It's a gentle spooky groove that makes you feel like the band is riding away over the horizon and into the night.

## Ten (Reissue)

In 2009 – two years before the album's 20th anniversary, for some reason, it was repackaged and re-released with great fanfare. This package contains so much extra material from Pearl Jam's 1991/1992 breakout era, that it deserves its own separate write-up.

With Pearl Jam – like for other bands – the fandom thrives by sharing rare and obscure recordings. Their lack of availability gives them a special aura, and knowledge of them is a kind of gnostic lore that distinguishes hardcore fans from casuals. The *Ten* reissue includes something for all levels of obsession. It gave long-term collectors high-quality copies of their most desired items, and it gave fans who weren't there at the start, the opportunity to appreciate the album's wider context.

The re-release came in four editions. The Super Deluxe edition includes the original album remastered, a complete digital remix, six previously unreleased bonus tracks, a DVD of Pearl Jam's 1992 *MTV Unplugged* performance, vinyl copies of both *Ten* and the remixed *Ten*, a double-vinyl of a Seattle concert from 20 September 1992 (dubbed *A Drop In The Park*), a replica cassette of the original three-song *Momma-Son* demo that begat 'Once, 'Alive' and 'Footsteps', a replica of Vedder's personal song notes, and sundry memorabilia. The Deluxe edition includes the two versions of *Ten* on CD, the bonus tracks and the *MTV Unplugged* DVD. The vinyl edition includes the two versions in LP form. Finally, the Legacy edition (the cheapest and most commonly available) includes just the two album versions on CD, with the six bonus tracks on CD 2.

The bonus element that's common across all four editions – and which formed the core of the reissue – is the album's remixed version. Rick Parashar's original production was considered by some to be too slick; too *arena rock*. That criticism has always seemed facile to me. If you play *Ten* alongside an actual arena-rock album from the same year – such as Guns N' Roses' *Use Your Illusion I* or Van Halen's *For Unlawful Carnal Knowledge* – it sounds as raw as John Lennon's *Plastic Ono Band* by comparison. But in 1991, *Ten* wasn't being compared to those albums; it was being compared to Nirvana's *Nevermind*, Soundgarden's *Badmotorfinger* and Mudhoney's *Every Good Boy Deserves Fudge*. Those albums retained some of the gritty unpolished feel of the original Seattle scene: music for sweaty local clubs rather than huge impersonal arenas. The relatively polished and spacious sound of *Ten*, rubbed some listeners the wrong way, and the band came to share that opinion. 'I'd love to remix *Ten*', Ament told *Spin* in 2001: 'Ed, for sure, would agree with me'.

So for the 2009 re-release, they asked record producer Brendan O'Brien to remix it. O'Brien had already had a dry run at this when he remixed the *Ten* songs that were included on Pearl Jam's 2006 greatest hits collection *Rearviewmirror*. O'Brien had mixed the original *Ten,* and mixed and/ or produced all of their albums up until the eponymous 2006 album. His participation makes the point of the project, plain: they didn't want to radically overhaul the album, they just want it to sound more like their other albums. Ament told *MSN* in 2009: 'When we made *Vs.*, our second record, I remember thinking, 'Man, I wish our first record sounded like this'. I thought it was more direct; more powerful. I know Stone felt that the reverb on *Ten* was covering up our own inability to play at the time, but when I found a tape of the rough mixes, it sounded killer'.

In general, O'Brien's remixes did two things: increase the separation between the instruments, and push Vedder's vocals to the front. It's a much drier mix, with less ambience and more immediacy. Sometimes the result is positive – 'Once' and 'Jeremy' sound even more intense, and on 'Even Flow' and 'Why Go', it's easier to appreciate Gossard's splashy rhythm work. Sometimes it's negative – without the sonic oomph, 'Even Flow' sounds a little lethargic, and the opening to 'Garden' now sounds too busy. Sometimes it's both – 'Alive' and 'Black' sound more intimate as if Vedder is singing directly to you, but they lack the original mix's larger-than-life atmosphere.

Was the remix experiment a success? Well, many fans prefer it: especially second-generation fans who came to the band long after *Ten*. I prefer the original, but the beauty of it is that we don't have to choose. Unlike some other bands who have entirely replaced their albums' classic mixes with remixes that sound very different, Pearl Jam offered this version as an alternative but kept the *real* version available because they understood how beloved it was. The real question, is would *Ten* have been such a runaway success if it had always sounded like this? I imagine so because the songs are still incredible. Probably the only difference in that parallel universe is that there would be a small contingent of early fans who were mad that the band didn't sound enough like Temple Of The Dog.

The major attraction of the Deluxe and Super Deluxe editions, is the inclusion of the band's never-before-commercially-available *MTV Unplugged* session in its entirety. Fans who saw the show when it was broadcast, for decades spoke of it with reverence, and it was heavily bootlegged. This release includes the entire concert on DVD, featuring a previously unissued performance of 'Oceans'. It was worth the wait for any fans who missed it the first time.

*MTV Unplugged* – a show where artists would perform a stripped-down acoustic concert in an intimate setting – is a real relic of the 1990s. It's strange that it was once considered a novel idea to rearrange electric rock songs for acoustic instruments. Underlying this was the implicit idea that music is somehow more *pure* and *real* if it's made without flash and embellishment. Critics these days sneer at such a rockist notion. But at the time, *Unplugged* was less about wanting to be seen as a *real artist*, and more about showing how your songs were so good that they could hold up without all the volume and effects.

Pearl Jam's *Unplugged* session was a perfect example of this. It demonstrated the quality of the band's writing. These songs sounded as great played on acoustic instruments as they did in an electrified setting. The highlight is undoubtedly 'Black': that one song has a career-making performance from Vedder. The band also played a song that would become a fan favourite when it was made widely available in its electric version three months after the special aired: 'State of Love And Trust' (See *Singles*). The only criticism of the set is that the drums are mixed quite high. Maybe that's because their new drummer Dave Abbruzzese (a flashier and more forceful player) played this concert. Coming from Dallas, Abbruzzese had been recommended to them by drummer

Matt Chamberlain, who had filled in for three weeks after Dave Krusen left. Krusen went on to join the underrated Seattle band Candlebox in 1997.

Abbruzzese was also on board for the *Drop In The Park* concert. This saw the band play every song from *Ten* except for 'Ocean', and 'State Of Love And Trust'. With so many live Pearl Jam albums now available, this is hardly an essential item, but it is worth hearing as a time capsule of the band rocking their hometown before they expanded their sound and their audience.

Beyond these items, the main reason you should trade in your original copy of *Ten* for the reissue is the otherwise unavailable bonus tracks. 'Breath And A Scream' and 'State Of Love And Trust' are demos of songs that would be released on the *Singles* soundtrack, and will be discussed in that entry.

### 'Brother' (Gossard, Vedder)

This is a song with a curious history. It's a thunderous fast guitar workout similar to 'Deep' and 'Porch'. You wouldn't think that such a song might've caused the band to break up before they began, but it came close! Apparently, Gossard grew uninterested in playing it. But Ament loved it, and Gossard's refusal sparked a blowout that almost lead to Ament quitting. Fortunately, things were patched up, but 'Brother' was left unreleased. That all seems inexplicable, as this is as good as any mid-tier Pearl Jam track from the era. It was released to radio to promote the *Ten* reissue, and actually topped the US Modern Rock chart for two weeks. It sounded like Gods of Olympus touching down compared to Shinedown and Seether.

### 'Just A Girl' (Gossard, Vedder)

This is a 1990 demo from when the band were still called Mookie Blaylock. It's the closest that early-Pearl Jam came to sounding like Soundgarden, due to the slightly off-kilter rhythm and the vaguely Middle Eastern riff (Compare to 'Fresh Tendrils' on Soundgarden's *Superunknown*). This demo could've developed into something interesting, but it doesn't feel like a missed opportunity.

### '2000 Mile Blues' (Ament, Krusen, McCready, Vedder)

This is a rarity in the Pearl Jam canon: a no-frills 12-bar blues. The band plod along like the world's most lethargic bar band, and Vedder mumbles and hollers his way through an unconvincing George Thorogood impression. We should all be grateful that they didn't pursue this direction any further. Blues rock's time in the mainstream spotlight died with Stevie Ray Vaughan, and in the 1990s, blues fans had the real deal – like Junior Kimbrough and R. L. Burnside – to listen to.

### 'Evil Little Goat' (Ament, Gossard, Krusen, McCready, Vedder)

A 90-second Cramps impression, wherein Vedder mumbles the title phrase in a half-arsed Elvis voice over a murky rockabilly riff.

# **Singles** (Soundtrack) (1992)

Personnel (for Pearl Jam's songs):
Dave Abbruzzese: drums
Jeff Ament: bass
Stone Gossard: rhythm guitar
Mike McCready: lead guitar
Eddie Vedder: vocals
Producer: Rick Parasher
Recorded at London Bridge studio in Seattle, Washington, January 1992
Release date: 30 June 1992
Chart places: US: 43
Running time: 65:27

The first new music Pearl Jam released after *Ten* was via the Ten Club: the fan club they set up in 1990. Every Christmas they issued collectable vinyl singles to the members (see The Ten Club holiday singles section). But the music that the wider public got to hear next, was on the soundtrack to the film *Singles*. Such was the impact of this film – or rather its soundtrack – that it's deserving of its own separate entry.

*Singles* is a 1992 romantic comedy, set and filmed in Seattle, documenting the relationship turmoils of a group of 20-something Gen-Xers. The none-more-1990s ensemble cast includes Campbell Scott, Bridget Fonda and Matt Dillon, who is a standout as the singer of an aspiring grunge band named Citizen Dick. Soundgarden and Alice In Chains perform in the film, and Vedder, Gossard and Ament have brief acting roles as the other members of Citizen Dick. The film isn't worth watching to see the members of Pearl Jam, but it is worth watching as a time capsule of its era.

*Singles* was written and directed by Cameron Crowe, who at age 35 already had a storied career in filmmaking *and* rock and roll. He started out at age 16 as a journalist for *Rolling Stone*, married Heart's Nancy Wilson, wrote the 1982 film *Fast Times At Ridgemont High*, and made the 1989 high school romance *Say Anything...*, which included Mother Love Bone's 'Chloe Dancer/Crown Of Thorns' on its soundtrack. Crowe was an early fan of the Seattle scene, and with *Singles,* he preserved something of it before the mass-media marketing machine invaded.

The movie helped define the new style dubbed 'grunge'. Almost overnight, out went the big hair, the fluorescent colours, the geometric patterns and other holdovers from 1980s fashion. In came plaid shirts, ripped jeans, confrontational slogans and unkempt facial hair. It was a paradox – the media rushing to capitalise on a music scene that prided itself on being anti-commercial, cynicism, and an idealised notion of authenticity. Despite being released amid this wave of hype, *Singles* wasn't a case of *grunge-sploitation*; it was a heartfelt tribute to the scene, and you can tell by the soundtrack Crowe assembled.

If an alien came to earth, put a gun to your head and demanded to know what grunge music is, you would play them a copy of the *Singles* soundtrack. Like *Saturday Night Fever* did for disco, it captures most of the major players and the full range of sounds in one eminently listenable package. It includes a new and/or otherwise-unavailable song by every major Seattle grunge band, aside from Nirvana. Their 'Smells Like Teen Spirit' *was* originally included in the film, but it had to be cut, as the song became a hit during production, and the royalty rate went up. So it's a miracle this soundtrack exists at all: it would've been massively more expensive to compile even a few months later.

The soundtrack opens with 'Would?' from Alice in Chains' upcoming magnum opus *Dirt*. Soundgarden contributed the thunderous 'Birth Ritual'; Chris Cornell released his first solo song: the gorgeous Zeppelin-esque 'Seasons'; Screaming Trees included their almost-hit 'Nearly Lost You', and Mudhoney called out the entire idea of a Seattle scene with 'Overblown'. Mother Love Bone's 'Chloe Dancer/Crown Of Thorns' was also included, finally finding the wide audience it always deserved. The soundtrack also helped situate the Seattle scene in the wider context of alternative rock at the time – there is the track 'Drown' by future superstars Smashing Pumpkins, and the first two solo songs from ex-Replacements icon Paul Westerberg. The soundtrack also helped bridge the new rock with classic rock, via the inclusion of Jimi Hendrix's 'May This Be Love' and an acoustic Led Zeppelin cover (The Battle Of Evermore) from Heart's Anne and Nancy Wilson as The Lovemongers.

Then of course there are Pearl Jam's two contributions, which became instant fan favourites. In 2017, the album was released with a bonus disc containing a host of unreleased recordings by most of the soundtrack artists *except* Pearl Jam. However, there is a recording of Citizen Dick performing the Mudhoney variation 'Touch Me I'm Dick'.

## 'Breath' (Gossard, Vedder)

A thick slow slab of a song, distinguished by a twin guitar riff with a watery tone. With its surging rise-and-fall dynamics, it feels like this song washes over you. 'Breath' dates back to Mother Love Bone, and it definitely would not have suited Andrew Wood's flamboyant vocal style. Pearl Jam recorded this song during the *Ten* sessions, and that version is included on the *Ten* reissue. There's little significant difference other than that this version feels a little tighter and cleaner. That may be because this was one of the first songs recorded with Pearl Jam's second drummer Dave Abbruzzese.

## 'State Of Love and Trust' (Ament, McCready, Vedder)

This was the fastest, hardest-hitting song Pearl Jam had released up to this point. It was also another one of the first to be recorded with Dave Abbruzzese, although, according to an interview with MSN, Ament prefers the early version they recorded with Krusen. Comparing that version (on the *Ten* reissue) to this, the main difference is the recording quality.

The inclusion of this song on the *Singles* soundtrack, seems like a pre-emptive move by the band, to assert their punk credentials. Remember that compared to the other artists on the soundtrack, Pearl Jam were relative neophytes; upstarts even. There is also nothing less punk than an easy-going rom-com, and while Vedder wrote these lyrics after watching an early cut, they're much darker and more intense than anything in the film itself. It immediately became a fixture in their live set, and it remains a favourite of fans who prefer the band's nastier side.

# Vs. (1993)

Personnel:
Dave Abbruzzese: drums
Jeff Ament: bass
Stone Gossard: rhythm guitar
Mike McCready: lead guitar
Eddie Vedder: vocals, rhythm guitar
Producer: Brendan O'Brien
Recorded at The Site, Nicasio, California, March-May 1993
Release date: 19 October 1993
Chart places: US: 1, UK: 2
Running time: 46:11

In many ways, the real story of Pearl Jam begins with their second album. As with many bands, in recording their debut, Pearl Jam used up all the songs they'd saved up from years of practising and playing live. So *Vs.* was their first album written largely from scratch. It was also their first album written entirely as a fully formed group, and was their first written with new drummer Dave Abbruzzese. Most importantly, it was written as a reaction to the unexpected success of *Ten*. While *Ten* still defines Pearl Jam in most people's minds, *Vs.* is when the band defined themselves. It's a mess of contradictions. It's rawer but more considered. It's more intense, but also more playful. It has more of a punk rock feel, yet it's also more eclectic. In short, it's the definitive Pearl Jam album.

If Pearl Jam had broken up after *Ten*, they would likely still be remembered as one of the great one-and-done bands in rock history, alongside Derek and the Dominoes, Sex Pistols, Rites Of Spring and The La's. But to have your debut album be your biggest hit – and not just that, but a defining album of your generation – is both a blessing and a curse. On the one hand, you've already secured your legacy and you're guaranteed a lifetime of royalties from at least one huge radio hit (see Boston, Supergrass, The Killers). On the other hand, you might never be able to escape the shadow of that early success, and you'll be trapped between trying to recapture it or trying to move beyond it (see Boston, Supergrass, The Killers). Pearl Jam could've tried to remake *Ten* again and again, and some of their fan base no doubt wished they had. But fortunately for the band, a large enough proportion of their fan base understood that the band couldn't do that and remain true to themselves.

*Vs.* is still undeniably a grunge album (though the band would deny the 'grunge' tag), but it includes elements that aren't typically associated with grunge, like funky bass lines and tribal drumming. They also brought acoustic instruments to the fore on many songs: a smart decision given the popularity of their *MTV Unplugged* session. They may also have been inspired by the recently released *Automatic For The People* by R.E.M.: a band looked to as an example of how to blow up commercially without selling out your principles.

Just like them, Pearl Jam were not happy to be confined to one genre, and their eclectic approach ensured that they would not be compared to Mudhoney for much longer. The overall message of *Vs.* is, 'We refuse to be what you expect us to be'. And they had reasons to fear being pigeonholed, given what happened in the aftermath of *Ten*'s release.

It can be overlooked these days, but *Ten* actually outsold Nirvana's *Nevermind*. But it was 'Smells Like Teen Spirit' that got tagged with the anthem-for-a-generation label. Kurt Cobain was elevated to the status of spokesman for the youth, and his opinion set the barometer for what was and wasn't considered cool. So, naturally, the music press pitted the two bands against each other. Cobain was not shy about coming forth with his opinion on Pearl Jam. He told the *Chicago Tribune* in 1991: 'But now there's a corporate tag on the Seattle scene, and I find it offensive to be lumped in with bands like Pearl Jam'. And to *Musician* magazine: 'I would love to be erased from my association with that band: the ones responsible for this corporate, alternative and cock-rock fusion'. He might've been uncharitable to Pearl Jam, but Cobain now seems uncannily prescient in his assessment of where music was headed.

Two bands fighting over who's the more *real*, makes for a fun rivalry. But when you have over a dozen bands with a similar sound and attitude getting drawn into the discussion, people start talking about a *new wave*. A *Time* magazine cover story published the week *Vs.* was released, sums it up: 'All The Rage', the headline blares, over a picture of Vedder screaming his lungs out: 'Angry young rockers like Pearl Jam give voice to the passions and fears of a generation'. People needed a label to group all these angry young rockers under, and thanks to record label Sub Pop's marketeers, 'grunge' became that label. And lo – critics, advertisers, A&R men, radio programmers and fans, started applying it willy-nilly.

Pearl Jam's Seattle brethren – Nirvana, Soundgarden, Alice In Chains, Mudhoney, Screaming Trees and poor overlooked Tad – constituted the first wave of grunge, along with just about every band that was or had been signed to Sup Pop records. One of these was L7, who paved the way for many female-fronted grunge bands, including Babes In Toyland, Hole and Veruca Salt. The remit was extended to more eclectic female-led bands like The Breeders and Belly, and it also allowed iconoclastic artists like PJ Harvey and Tori Amos to get a foot in the door.

The grunge label was also applied to bands from outside Seattle who shared some elements – if they used a lot of distortion and minor keys; if they could not be easily classified as punk or metal; if they had a grotty, scrappy look and an anti-mainstream attitude; if they had a vocalist with either a whiny abrasive voice or a resonant baritone, they were dubbed 'grunge'. This includes Chicago's Smashing Pumpkins, whose debut was released before *Ten*, but whose second album *Siamese Dream* was released in July 1993 to a rapturous reception. There was also The Afghan Whigs from Cincinnati, The Jesus Lizard from Austin, and The Lemonheads from Boston. All these bands were active before *Ten* was released, but then alt-rock bands that had influenced the Seattle scene (Sonic Youth, Dinosaur Jr., Pixies, Melvins) were grandfathered into the new genre.

There was a danger of Pearl Jam's unique qualities getting overlooked in this rush. In the aftermath of *Ten,* came Seattle's B team: bands such as My Sister's Machine, Love Battery and Gruntruck (Yes, those are all real band names). These bands never made it big, but they still delivered quality albums, all of which sounded much more like Pearl Jam than the underground music that originally informed the Seattle scene. Then there were bands that – rightly or wrongly – got tagged by the press as blatant Pearl Jam imitators: there was San Diego's Stone Temple Pilots, whose breakthrough single 'Plush' could've been a *Ten* outtake. Pennsylvania's Live sounded like a lab-engineered hybrid of Pearl Jam and R.E.M.. Anyone who wanted 'Pearl Jam by numbers', could turn to these bands.

So it's no surprise that there was a backlash from the band, towards the grunge label and its connotations. 'There's so much hype, you could choke on it', Gossard told the *Los Angeles Times* in 1992: 'I wish people would forget that we come from Seattle'. It's also no surprise that there was a backlash against the *band*. They were regarded as Johnny-come-latelys, or worse: industry plants. Kurt Cobain summed this attitude up. He told *Rolling Stone* that he felt 'a duty to warn kids about false music that's claiming to be underground or alternative'. This backlash made Pearl Jam more desperate to prove to their audience – and perhaps to themselves – that they were their own men. Vedder in particular was self-conscious about his image, and no wonder, after being unwillingly anointed by the press as the face of grunge. He said to *Spin* in 2001: 'I never knew that someone could put you on the cover of a magazine without asking you; that they could sell magazines and make money, and you didn't have a copyright on your face or something'. As a result, he and the band adopted a staunchly anti-fame attitude. Said Gossard in that same interview: '(Vedder) immediately realised that getting bigger wasn't necessarily going to make any of us any happier'.

They put their money where their mouths were in one respect: they made no music videos to promote the singles from *Vs.* That might not seem like a big deal, but in the 1990s, getting an eye-catching music video in regular MTV rotation could make a band's fortunes. Moreover, music videos were accepted as their own kind of legitimate art form. But for older rock fans, they were still seen as glorified advertisements, better suited for pop acts whose music didn't have enough substance to stand on its own. Pearl Jam regarded videos as a distraction they resented being expected to do. They had the old-school mentality where it's supposed to be all about the music: 'I don't want people to remember our songs as videos', Ament told *Rolling Stone* in 1993.

Looking back, there seems something churlish – even childish – about Pearl Jam's negative attitude to their own fame. Today, a band that sold even a quarter of the units that *Vs.* did, would be crowned the saviours of rock music.

At the time, many people rolled their eyes at Pearl Jam's attitude, and likely would've dismissed the band entirely if they hadn't used this attitude as fuel to write some of the best songs of their career.

The band's motto while they were making this album was 'Five against one': a statement of unity in opposition. The phrase appears in the lyrics of 'Animal', and in the CD booklet, there's a picture of it written on the palm of a hand. It was also to have been the name of the album, but that was changed to *Vs.* to reflect the state of conflict that the band felt they were constantly in. The title is attention-grabbing in its brevity, and it evokes a general all-purpose sense of dissatisfaction. It also fits the cover art: an extreme close-up of a sheep snarling as it strains against a wire fence. The booklet includes more confrontational imagery, such as a demonic mask hidden among the weeds, and the naked torso with the song titles written on it. Once more, the lyrics are handwritten and often incomplete. There are cute touches, like the words for 'Glorified G' written inside a giant G. This time, hand-drawn sketches – of guns and needles – accompanied the lyrics. In some ways, the booklet resembles a serial killer's journal more than album liner notes!

In the end, the album's packaging was irrelevant, because the music did the talking. A major factor in that, was the band's new producer Brendan O'Brien. I say 'new', but O'Brien had mixed both *Temple Of The Dog* and *Ten*. He had also engineered and/or mixed albums such as The Black Crowes' *Shake Your Money Maker*, Red Hot Chili Peppers' *Blood Sugar Sex Magick* and The Jayhawks' *Hollywood Town Hall*: all of which balanced hard-rocking oomph with moments of sensitivity and grace. O'Brien's first success as a producer was Stone Temple Pilot's debut *Core*: the most *Ten* sounding album that isn't *Ten*. He was definitely the right man for the job: so much so that he became Pearl Jam's default producer for the following decade and a half.

When *Vs.* was released on 19 October 1993, it set a record, selling almost 1,000,000 copies in its first five days of release. That week, it outperformed all other entries in the *Billboard* top 10 combined and reached number 1 in most of the English-speaking world. This is an even more remarkable achievement considering that none of the album's singles made it to the pop charts. This album owed its success to the millions of fans who were hungry to hear what Pearl Jam had to say. And they had plenty to say.

## 'Go' (Abbruzzese, Vedder)

The band tease the listeners with 30 seconds of tuning up and false starts – mixed to sound like they're playing in the room next door and you're hearing them through the wall. Anybody who cranks up the volume to hear it more clearly, is in for a rude shock when a four-note riff slams in like the band is beating down your door. This song brings Pearl Jam's punk influences firmly to the fore. It's short and breathlessly fast, to the point where Vedder seems to struggle to fit all his words in. It also has a much drier sound. The guitars and bass are blended together into an ominous rumble, like supercharged surf rock. Abbruzzese makes his presence felt immediately; his drumming has a funky snap that really makes the music *move*. A lot of punk rock is just aggression for aggression's sake, but not here.

While this song title is ideal for an album opener, it has a darker meaning in the context of the lyrics. 'Please don't go on me,' goes the chorus. But this isn't a romantic song: it's sung from the perspective of an abuser begging their partner not to leave them. The key line – sung by Vedder with such fury that it's hard to make out – is 'Supposed I abused you?/Just passing it on'. This is a song about the cycle of abuse; how abused people can turn into abusers, and use their past treatment as an excuse for their bad behaviour. The theme of escaping abuse is all over this album. It's a far cry from Guns N' Roses' 'Back Off Bitch'.

As a clear statement of intent, this was released as the album's first single. It came nowhere near the mainstream chart, but it was a hit on US rock radio. It also reached number 5 in Norway, and 2 in New Zealand! That's evidence that Pearl Jam were a global phenomenon.

## 'Animal' (Gossard, Vedder)

This gets my vote for Pearl Jam's best pure hard-rocker. That's a bold claim to be sure; nothing beats the precision and efficiency of this ensemble performance. 'Animal' is the best example of the power these men are able to generate using the basic tools of rock music. No frills, no fluff, just an absolute monster of a riff. The guitar tone is so crisp, and the playing so precise, that it feels as if every note is hammering your ears.

This is almost like an answer song to 'Go'. Vedder sings from the perspective of someone in an abusive relationship: 'Why would you want to hurt me?', he screams. As if to make the point clear that this is a song of empathic rage and not another fist-pumping jock-rock anthem, the chorus is quieter than the rest of the song. The main riff gives way to a funk-metal breakdown, as Vedder audibly seethes, 'I'd rather be with an animal'. Then the riff comes slamming back in. It's a masterful use of dynamics.

This was released as the album's third single, and predictably flopped everywhere except in New Zealand, where it reached seven in the pop charts.

## 'Daughter' (Gossard, Vedder)

One of the things that was overlooked in all the talk of Vedder's white male rage, was that he often wrote from the perspective of vulnerable women, with a sense of empathy that many of his contemporaries lacked. Kurt Cobain did this in songs such as 'Polly', but there was a voyeuristic element to his lyrics that isn't present in Vedder's. As often as he wrote about domestic abuse and mental illness, he also wrote about quiet moments of interpersonal drama. This song is the first and best example of that.

I had always thought the song was about a girl who's lost one or both parents, and she resents her new mother's attempts to bond with her. 'Don't call me daughter, not fit to/The picture kept will remind me'. But Vedder clarified in 1995 that it's about a child with a learning difficultly ('Mother reads aloud, child tries to understand') and how the parents don't understand this, and punish her for it. That is hinted at in the line 'She holds the hand that holds her down'. This reading gives a sinister edge to the coda, where Vedder distantly repeats 'The shades go down'.

The music is just as striking as the lyrics, being their first acoustic song. It has touches of country, but sounds nothing like alt-country, which was just making its presence known at the time via bands like Uncle Tupelo and The Jayhawks. 'Daughter' harkens back to the Americana of the 1970s; to observational singer-songwriters like John Prine. The opening acoustic riff is one of the most recognisable in Pearl Jam's discography, and it sets the down-home small-town mood. McCready's guitar solo – apparently one of the first he had to sit down and properly compose – is the song's sole moment of escapism, when it feels like the girl might break free. Then the song winds down slowly with a sharp, almost bluegrass style guitar/bass interplay.

This was released as the album's second single, and was the most successful. It reached number 1 on the US rock radio charts and made the top 20 on the pop charts throughout Europe and Australasia. It remains a cornerstone of Pearl Jam's setlists. On stage, this coda became another launching point for improvisation, and for the band to work in snatches of other songs. A good example of this is their 16 April 1994 performance on *Saturday Night Live*. This took place soon after Kurt Cobain's death, and the band incorporated Neil Young's 'Hey Hey, My My (Into The Black)': the song Cobain quoted in his suicide note. This performance is available on YouTube if you fancy a good cry.

## 'Glorified G' (Gossard, McCready, Vedder)

This is one of the album's lesser songs, but at least it's memorable. It's a sparsely arranged track, based around a grinding riff that's so compressed it sounds almost comical, as if the guitar was blowing a raspberry. That fits, because for the first time, Vedder sings from the perspective of a caricature rather than a character. The lyrics could not be more obvious about their target: gun nuts. The recurring line 'glorified version of a pellet gun', makes no bones about what the band thinks of Second Amendment obsessives. In some ways, this song is the thematic flip side of 'Jeremy': there's no sympathy in this portrait of a man who's just itching to use his gun against other people.

## 'Dissident' (Ament, Gossard, McCready, Vedder)

If there was any justice, this song would've topped the charts everywhere and become an anthem to rival 'Alive'. The main guitar part is a blues lick so simple and effective that Billy Gibbons or Joe Perry could've written it. But the combined powers of the band (This was written by all five members) elevate it to a higher level. Abbruzzese's swinging rhythm gives the track a woozy off-kilter feel, which fits the story's paranoid feel. Vedder's lyric tells of a man – a freedom fighter for an unspecified cause – who takes shelter with a woman. Unable to handle the pressure, she gives him up to the authorities. 'She couldn't hold on,' goes the chorus. 'Oh, she folded'. The middle eight, ratchets up the tension for the devastating final verse on which Vedder's anguish is palpable. It's clear he has sympathy for the woman; not everyone is cut out to be a rebel.

### 'W.M.A.' (Abbruzzese, Ament, Vedder)

This song is the first gonzo risk on the album: musically and lyrically. The title stands for 'White Male America', which means that Pearl Jam were discussing the concept of social privilege long before the term became a buzzphrase. Vedder's lyrics are impressionistic descriptions – 'He won the lottery when he was born'; 'Do no wrong, so clean-cut'; 'Dirty his hands it come right off'. It quickly becomes clear that he's singing about a 'po-lice man', as the chorus goes.

This song was inspired by an incident where the police harassed a black friend of Vedder's, while they left him alone. This song isn't about that incident specifically, but about how racism allows white officers to get away with violence against black people. The shadow of the Rodney King trial and the L.A. riots, hangs over this song. But in the booklet, the band included a photo of Malice Green: an unarmed black man who was beaten to death by white police officers in 1992. Green's murderers were actually convicted. Like 'Glorified G', this song is, alarmingly, still relevant.

Musically, this sounds like nothing the band has done before or since, or like what anyone else was making at the time. It's like a combination of noise rock, funk and Afrobeat. The closest comparison is early Public Image Ltd. – Ament's hummable bass line is reminiscent of Jah Wobble's dub-style playing. And as with Keith Levene, the guitar is used for texture rather than to drive the song along. Abbruzzese deserves the bulk of the credit though – the main feature of this track is his relentless pattern that runs through the entire song, rising and falling in intensity. It sounds like 1000 jackboots stomping in unison.

### 'Blood' (Gossard, McCready, Vedder)

This rocker is a less-well-realised cousin of 'Animal', being a single simple riff that's flogged to death. Its only distinguishing musical element is the lashings of wah-wah guitar. Lyrically, it compares intravenous drug use to media intrusion. You can tell this by the booklet's extremely subtle illustration with a needle and a fountain pen both dripping blood. It's clear from Vedder's especially unhinged performance, that he doesn't think much of either practice. His long raspy scream after the second chorus is bone-chilling.

### 'Rearviewmirror' (Vedder)

This is the album's fan favourite, evidenced by the fact that it lent its name to the band's greatest hits album. It immediately became a live fixture, to the point that it's known simply as 'RVM' on setlists. It's a song designed to hype up a crowd, with its catchy minor-key rockabilly riff that never lets up as the music builds in intensity towards an explosive catharsis.

More than the music though, it's the lyric that connected with fans. For the first time on this album, Vedder is singing from a place of vulnerability rather than defence. Coming immediately after the histrionics of 'Blood', the difference is striking. Rather than screaming and bellowing as he had for most of the album to this point, here he sings in a measured matter-of-fact way, making his feeling clear in no uncertain terms. Despite its punky sound, this is a song in the grand tradition of Bruce Springsteen's 'Thunder Road' (and 'Born To Run' and 'Badlands' *et al.*): about that longing to escape your hometown. But Vedder adds an element of the bitterness that Springsteen usually saved for his acoustic albums. Vedder explicitly states that he's leaving behind physical and emotional abuse. But a listener doesn't have to have suffered similarly to relate to the feeling of release this song evokes. Anyone who has found the strength to leave behind a bad relationship, a bad friendship, a bad job, can relate to Vedder's climactic cry: 'Saw things so much clearer once you were in my rearview mirror'.

### 'Rats' (Ament, Vedder)

This is another funk song, but compared to 'W.M.A.', this is more *fun*, if that last word could be applied to a song that compares humans unfavourably to rats. What elevates this song, is Vedder's verse vocals: he's halfway to rapping. For maximum ironic appeal, the fade-out features a snatch of Michael Jackson's old weepie 'Ben', which was – lest we forget – a song written for a horror film about a boy who befriends a killer rat.

While this song is unlikely to be anybody's favourite on the album, it's another example of the band's musical chemistry.

### 'Elderly Woman Behind The Counter In A Small Town' (Vedder)

This song has the longest title of any Pearl Jam song – apparently, that was intentional: the band going against their propensity for single-word titles. It's one of the band's most unassuming songs. If 'Daughter' was a step sideways into roots rock, this sounds more like a long-lost folk standard; something itinerant workers could sing around a campfire. It has that guileless feel because it was written by Vedder in a sudden burst of inspiration. Open D, G, and C major chords give the song a bighearted sound. It feels like a spontaneous outpouring of emotion.

It's so charming that it's possible to overlook the sad nature of the lyrics. The woman of the title, recognises a customer as an old flame, but is afraid to say hello when she notes how well he's doing for himself and how little *she* has changed. At its heart, this is another Springsteen-esque song about small-town life, except this time the main character has missed her chance to escape. The song winds down with the melancholy refrain 'Hearts and thoughts, they fade, fade away'. In concert, this became a sing-along; it's ironic that an expression of helpless regret became a big communal moment, but that's the magic of Pearl Jam. The original and the live version from *Live On Two Legs* both became rock-radio hits.

### 'Leash' (Gossard, McCready, Vedder)

This is the album's final hard rocker, and it sounds awkward jammed between two more low-key songs. While it's no lost gem, 'Leash' repays repeated listenings. The chaotic opening makes it feel like this will be the most punky song on the album, but then the chorus slows down and it seems like the band is relaxing their guard; then the climax hits and fair takes your head off. This is apparently about the same girl Vedder wrote of in 'Why Go'. In this case, it's sung from her perspective, as she lashes out at her oppressive, restrictive family: hence the climactic plea of 'Drop the leash!'. The line 'Get out of my fucking face' is written in the booklet as 'lucky face', perhaps to avoid the wrath of the censor.

### 'Indifference' (Ament, Gossard, Vedder)

Compared to the cathartic 'Release' on *Ten*, this album closer is a far more bleak note to end on. 'Release' is the sound of a man asserting his will to freedom; 'Indifference' is the sound of a man who has all but given up. 'How much difference does it make?', asks the chorus. The real question is, who is trying to make a difference to what? The lyrics don't give an answer: doubly so because they aren't printed in the booklet. It's almost an admission of defeat. But then Vedder sings, 'I will hold the candle until it burns up my arm/I will take their punches until their arm grows tired'. Who is 'they'? It's tempting to say that it's the press, the intrusive fans, the musical gatekeepers. Vedder sounds like he's already sick of fighting them, but – in the words of a Tom Petty song, the band would cover on the *Vs.* tour – he 'won't back down'.

The organ (uncredited) gives the song a late-night feel. The distant bells make it feel as if the band is being marched against their will into the grey twilight. This is the halfway point between Black Sabbath's 'Planet Caravan' and Elvis Presley's cover of Bob Dylan's 'Tomorrow Is A Long Time': the song of a weary wanderer travelling to parts unknown.

'How much difference does it make' is a depressing thought for a song that became one of their most frequent show closers. The fact that such a despondent, introspective song is considered a good note to end a concert on, is a testament to the faith Pearl Jam have in their fans, to appreciate great music over empty fan service.

### Vs. (Reissue bonus tracks)

In 2011 – again, not the album's actual anniversary –*Vs.* and *Vitalogy* were re-released as a combined package with a variety of extras. The major draw for collectors is a concert from the *Vs.* tour – in Boston on 12 April 1994 – that previewed some songs from *Vitalogy*. The Limited-Edition Collector's Box Set includes an 'Exclusive collector's cassette featuring live tribute and studio performances from a number of Pearl Jam's fellow artist friends' – so no rare or undiscovered Pearl Jam gems there.

*Vs.* and *Vitalogy* each included bonus tracks. Now that the reissued editions of these are available separately, I'll address the bonus tracks separately. *Vs.* included an acoustic demo of 'Hold On': a song I'll discuss in the entry for *Lost Dogs*. That leaves two tracks.

## 'Cready Stomp' (McCready)

This instrumental studio outtake sounds like a fully-formed song that only needed lyrics. It's no great shakes tune-wise, but the players are firing on all cylinders. Musically, it's closer to *Ten* than to *Vs.*, but it could have replaced 'Glorified G' with no harm done.

## 'Crazy Mary' (Williams)

This is a cover of a song by American singer-songwriter Victoria Williams. Williams debuted in 1987 and was working her way out of cult status when she was diagnosed with multiple sclerosis. A host of alt-rock artists recorded an album of her songs to cover her medical expenses. The album was called *Sweet Relief*, and that title became the name of a non-profit charity that aids musicians in need of medical care.

Pearl Jam's contribution to the album was this spooky character portrait. It's a ripe slice of American gothic: an old woman who lives alone on the outskirts of town is killed by a car that goes off the road into her shack. The chorus – 'Take a bottle, drink it down, pass it around' – reflects the need for people to do something, anything, to cope with the fickle finger of fate.

The band's arrangement doesn't vary much from William's original. Vedder sings with a slight nasal affectation that sounds odd. He might've done this to blend better with Williams' backing vocals. At first, it sounds awkward, but eventually, their two voices blend harmoniously.

Bizarrely, this unassuming compilation contribution became a live favourite. It's the third-most-played cover song in Pearl Jam's repertoire, and it's usually extended to almost ten minutes, with guitar and organ solos. The ringing chord that opens the song is now greeted with cheers as big as for any original Pearl Jam song. Why this is especially odd, is that until this reissue, 'Crazy Mary' wasn't included on any Pearl Jam release. The only place to find the studio version of this cover was on the original *Sweet Relief* CD, which wasn't re-released until 2020. If you can find a copy of the compilation, it's worth owning, and not just for Pearl Jam's inclusion. It features the cream of early-1990s alt-country (The Jayhawks, Lucinda Williams, Buffalo Tom), and it shows what a talented songwriter Victoria Williams is.

# Vitalogy (1994)

Personnel:
Dave Abbruzzese: drums
Jeff Ament: bass
Stone Gossard: guitar, mellotron, backing vocals
Mike McCready: guitar
Eddie Vedder: lead vocals, guitar, accordion
With:
Brendan O'Brien: piano, pipe organ, Hammond organ
Jack Irons: drums on 'Hey Foxymophandlemama, That's Me'
Jimmy Shoaf: drums on 'Satan's Bed'
Producer: Brendan O'Brien
Recorded at Kingsway, New Orleans; Southern Tracks, Atlanta; Doppler, Atlanta;
Bad Animals, Seattle, November 1993-October 1994
Release date: 22 November 1994
Chart places: US: 1, UK: 4
Running time: 55:09

*Vs.* was the fastest-selling album in history: a remarkable achievement to be sure. But this was more of a reflection on *Ten* than *Vs.*: people bought Pearl Jam's second album because they liked their first. The *real* test of the band's longevity would be the reception to their second album. There are many examples of bands that landed with an incredible debut but followed it with an underwhelming effort, causing their third album to flounder and their career to stall. Think Television, The Stone Roses, The Strokes, MGMT, and many others now lost to history. Pearl Jam avoided the classic mistake of their second album being a virtual xerox of their first, but that left the possibility that people could reject their new sound. If so, they wouldn't pluck down money for the third album. So, *Vitalogy* was Pearl Jam's real make-or-break moment.

As it turned out, people really liked *Vs.*, because *Vitalogy* became the *second*-fastest-selling album of all time after *Vs.*! It was also the fastest-selling new vinyl record for the whole of the 1990s and 2000s, until Jack White's *Lazaretto* album in 2014 (and White had to include all sorts of gimmicky bells and whistles on that vinyl to get those sales). Buying new vinyl in 1994 was a relatively niche hobby, and this says something about Pearl Jam's core fandom: that a large portion of them are, for lack of a better term, music snobs. This is not a bad thing. In fact, it might've done Pearl Jam's career some good, because, if nothing else, *Vitalogy* is the kind of album that appeals to a particularly intransigent contrarian mindset.

No bones about it, *Vitalogy* is as strange an album to top the pop charts as you're likely to find. And it was deliberately strange, as if the band was testing their audience's commitment. At the time, that seemed like obstinate self-sabotage. In retrospect, it seems more like the band were playing the long con, for *Vitalogy* is an album that fans enjoy *because* of – not in spite of – its flaws. It's frequently ranked near the top of their discography, but rarely at the top; it's too much of a deliberate mess for such unconditional love. *Vitalogy* includes a Grammy-winning song, a huge crossover hit, and one of their great fan favourites. But it also includes a few throwaway sketches, an unlistenable sound collage, and their very worst conventional song.

There are various reasons for the album's haphazard feel. Many of the songs were written while the band were touring *Vs.*,and recorded during gaps in their schedule; McCready went to rehab for cocaine and alcohol abuse during the album's production. Intra-band communication was at an all-time low: Gossard stopped acting as mediator, and Vedder asserted himself as the final decision-maker. 'Benevolent dictatorship', McCready called it in *Spin*. The relationship between Abbruzzese and the rest of the band was hanging by a thread due to personality clashes, and by the time the album was finished, he was gone from the band.

Not content with only fighting themselves, the band also chose to pick a fight with one of the hands that fed them: ticket vendor Ticketmaster. The band were incensed when they discovered that Ticketmaster charged exorbitant service fees on every ticket, even for charity concerts. And so began a quixotic battle. The band tried to rearrange their tour to play venues that Ticketmaster didn't control, but that proved to be impossible. Ament and Gossard even testified before Congress about the company's exploitative monopoly. But 'twas all for naught. They had to settle for cancelling their 1994 summer tour, in protest. Their crusade against price-gouging was undeniably heroic, but – along with their continued refusal to make videos – it curtailed their rise in popularity. Moreover, the way the music press reported it, made Pearl Jam seem like humourless social-justice scolds, only a few distortion pedals away from U2.

Even worse than the Ticketmaster debacle though, was the 8 April 1994 death of Kurt Cobain, by suicide. This was a massive blow to the culture. In terms of premature rock star deaths, only Jimi Hendrix's could compare in terms of how much at the height of their powers they both seemed, and how much potential they seemed to leave unrealised. The difference was that Cobain took his own life rather than dying accidentally: a tragedy on a whole other level. Cobain's history with drugs was obviously a factor in his death, and Pearl Jam were intimately familiar with that problem, viz., Andrew Wood. But the fact that Cobain specifically mentioned the pressures of stardom in his farewell note, and that he didn't feel like an authentic rock star, weighed heavily on Vedder. He said to *Melody Maker*: 'People like him and me, we can't be real… We have to live up to the expectations of a million people. And we can't do that. And then there's a cynical fuckin' media on top of that'. Between Ticketmaster, the media and Cobain's death, it's no wonder Vedder felt the need to scream.

More so even than *Vs.*, *Vitalogy* is informed by the uneasy relationship the band had with their fame. Never has a band so embodied the zeitgeist while struggling to keep themselves so far away from it. People tend to cite the follow-up *No Code* as the moment Pearl Jam definitively broke away from the mainstream, but I would argue that *No Code*'s relatively lukewarm sales were because *Vitalogy* had already separated the fair-weather fans from the true believers. On *Vitalogy,* Pearl Jam became the band that critics accused them of being: po-faced would-be iconoclasts with a persecution complex. Even the *joke* tracks sound humourless. And yet, they were just so on top of their game at this point, that even having hobbled themselves, they delivered the goods. Stripped down to a ten-track 40-minute album of only the *proper* songs, this would've been a sure-fire crowd-pleaser. But who would want to strip it of its idiosyncratic weirdness?

The weirdness extends to the packaging. The title and theme come from an early-20th-century book of outdated medical information, that Vedder found at a garage sale. 'Vitalogy' means 'study of life', and *Life* was the album's original title. The booklet includes handwritten or typed lyrics: often incomplete or obscured. Interspersed amongst them are excerpts from the old book, with hilarious and sometimes worrying medical advice. There are also random photos and a copy of a petition protesting the murder of abortion doctors. The booklet as a whole is absorbing and disturbing: a great example of found art.

After a months-long delay caused by the Ticketmaster battle and problems with Epic Records, *Vitalogy* was released on 22 November 1994. It topped the charts in the US, the UK, Australia and New Zealand, and reached the top 10 throughout most of Europe (except for France). In the long term, it sold about as well globally as *Vs.* did: multiplatinum in multiple markets. It seemed – to their possible chagrin – that Pearl Jam were likely to remain rock stars for the foreseeable future.

### 'Last Exit' (Abbruzzese, Ament, Gossard, McCready, Vedder)

For the second time in a row, a Pearl Jam album opens with the sound of the band warming up. Compared to the bubbling intensity of the *Vs.* false start, this feels more like the band is granting the listener a peak behind the curtain before the show starts. This song is not particularly distinctive compared to their other album openers; it functions more like a prelude. It's effective in that it's utterly relentless and bleak, which sets the tone for the album. The opening drum rhythm is so primal, and the guitar riff so artless, that it feels atavistic, as if the band is reverting to its primordial form, which was surely the point. The lyrics are impressionistic snatches that connote a sense of the world rushing by and time running out. Vedder's climactic cry sounds damaging and raw.

### 'Spin The Black Circle' (Gossard, Vedder)

This was the first single from *Vitalogy,* and it set the mood for the album in no uncertain terms: dark, dense, intense. Unlike 'Go' – the first single from *Vs.* – which took a while to warm up, 'Spin the Black Circle' spends barely four seconds introducing itself before Gossard's pulverising descending riff kicks in. There's none of the fleet-footed funk that Abbruzzese brought to 'Go';

this is as pure a punk song as the band ever wrote. Which is odd because it's an ode to vinyl. There's something almost comical about it. Vedder sings *so* aggressively about his love of vinyl, that it sounds more like he's railing against this malignant force that has a hold on him. For those who collect vinyl, it can sometimes feel that way. In 1994, vinyl was considered a dead format, so this song was something of an anti-modernist statement. But how times have changed – according to the website Discogs, an original 1994 vinyl edition of *Vitalogy* can trade hands for as high as $224 US.

At the 1996 Grammy awards, 'Spin the Black Circle' won Best Hard Rock Performance: Pearl Jam's first Grammy. During the band's acceptance speech, Vedder said, 'I don't know what this means. I don't think it means anything'. This quote was immediately interpreted in bad faith as an example of Vedder's lack of gratitude to the music industry machinery that helped make him a star. It does come off that way, but his point was, in the long run, it's not awards and sales that matter, it's the music.

## 'Not For You' (Vedder)

I would not be surprised if this song is what made Neil Young decide to record with Pearl Jam (see *Mirror Ball/Merkin Ball*). It sounds like something he could've recorded with Crazy Horse. Like many of their best songs – such as 'Like A Hurricane' and 'Cinnamon Girl' – it seems like a simple thrash. But underneath the noise, there's a masterful command of texture and dynamics. 'Not For You' opens with a steady stomping Zeppelin-esque drum rhythm and an ominous guitar riff that seems to continuously build without ever resolving. This riff rises and falls in intensity as they layer on squalls of feedback, while the rhythm never fully lets up. You keep expecting the song to explode into a full-on thrash metal rager, but it never does, and that makes it the more powerful.

Normally when a band hits on a groove like this, you'd describe them as 'cookin'' (or 'chooglin'' if you were Creedence Clearwater Revival). But the only word to describe this song, is 'seething'. It's directed at the number-one enemy of all alt-rock bands: the music industry. Specifically, it's about how record labels milk bands dry, as if the music was theirs. When Vedder screams 'This is not for you/It never was for you', he's talking to the parasitic marketers and merchandisers that exploit their music for profit. In retrospect, this is a naive view. These days rock fans would be amazed if a record label gave a fledgling band a tenth of the marketing push they once gave Pearl Jam. But that isn't the point. We know who it isn't for. But just who is Pearl Jam's music for? The fans of course.

## 'Tremor Christ' (Ament, McCready, Vedder)

This song was first released to the public on the 'Spin The Black Circle' single, and it has the feel of a B-side. That's not to say it's bad; more that it sounds like a demo. The spine of the song is a four-note riff that's perhaps the most simple Pearl Jam have yet written. It's so basic, that it hits the ear wrong. It feels as if there should be another riff interlocking with it. The song's woozy sound, coupled with reference to sailors and storms, makes it feel like a demented sea shanty.

### 'Nothingman' (Ament, Vedder)

The album's first ballad feels like a ray of sunlight peeking out from behind the clouds. That's despite the song's glum subject matter. It's a song of regret for a life wasted, about a man who failed to make the most of what he had. The key lines are 'Caught a bolt of lightning/Cursed the day he let it go'. It's a metaphor for a failed relationship: we can never know when love will strike us, and once gone it won't strike again. Ament was responsible for the music, which explains the lovely thick bass chords that hearken back to 'Black'.

This song showcases Vedder's lyric writing at its sensitive best, and his vocal is the perfect balance of sympathy and admonishment. The bridge is one of the most powerful moments on the record, culminating in the moment the drums and bass drop out, and – over a solitary guitar – Vedder cries 'Into the sun'. It manages to feel cathartic and miserable at the same time.

### 'Whipping' (Vedder)

Pulverising double-time drums and guitar lashes that do indeed sound like whips striking, lead this furious punk song. Once again, the chorus is quieter than the verses, but no less angry. Vedder hisses 'They're whipping' over and over. Like with 'Leash', the title is a metaphor for emotional abuse. But who's whipping who? It's unclear. The verses all begin with the word 'Don't': 'Don't need a helmet', 'Don't need a hand', 'Don't mean to push'. These are the words of a man who feels he's under attack. But it also implies he's not doing much to protect himself or accept help. It's a powerful piece of music, if not a particularly interesting song.

### 'Pry, To' (Abbruzzese, Ament, Gossard, McCready, Vedder)

This is a minute-long goof that fades in and away without leaving much impression. Vedder tunelessly wails 'P-R-I-V-A-C-Y'. Vedder was not alone among rock stars in wanting to guard his personal life from hostile prying eyes. In fact, that was a recurring theme in grunge, and was the main topic of some of the era's greatest songs, such as Nirvana's 'All Apologies' and Alice In Chains' 'Nutshell'. But Vedder is so literal here that it sounds petulant.

### 'Corduroy' (Vedder)

Like David Bowie's *Aladdin Sane* and The Police's *Synchronicity*, *Vitalogy* is an album that could've benefited from a reordered tracklist. There's no reason this absolute monster of a track should usher in the back half of the album, sandwiched in between a trifle and Pearl Jam's worst song. I understand that Pearl Jam wanted to make a statement with 'Spin the Black Circle', but if any song seemed designed to set the tone and theme of this album, it's 'Corduroy'. But no matter, because in the long run, this song set the tone and theme for the band's ongoing career.

It opens with a dreamlike cyclical guitar figure that rises up out of the silence while some melodic bass noodling builds tension. Then the song explodes into a powerful three-chord descending riff as Vedder enters. The song alternates these heavy verses with a lighter chorus wherein a minor chord adds an element of ambivalence, and that tension is the song's genius trick. This is Vedder's definitive statement about his own fame, and by extension, about the band's relationship with their fans.

The title refers to the cheap brown jacket that Vedder wore. He found that replicas of the jacket were being sold for hundreds of dollars. Even worse – it or similar clothing had become the default costume for characters in film and TV playing the Eddie Vedder type. It's one thing for your music to be bought and sold; it's another for your actual personality to be commodified. Vedder found it distressing that random elements of his authentic persona could be co-opted as a way to make money. In the chorus, he calls out the people responsible: 'I don't want to be help in your debt' and 'I don't want to take what you can give/I would rather starve than eat your bread' (Echoes of 'Hunger Strike' in that line). On first listen, it sounds like he's calling out his fans, or at least the kind of fan who would spend hundreds of dollars on a replica of his jacket. But the key line is tucked away in the bridge: 'Take my hand, not my picture'. He wants a genuine relationship with his fans, not something mediated through consumerism. 'Can't buy what I want because it's free', he cries at the song's climax. True human connection cannot be bought and sold the way merchandise can.

It's no wonder that fans zeroed in on 'Corduroy'. It summarises everything they love about the band – their individualist attitude, their open-hearted honesty and their sense of striving for something better: all coupled with their ability to make musical magic out of the simplest of ingredients. Without being released as a single, 'Corduroy' charted on US rock radio. It also became a concert centrepiece. It's their most played non-*Ten* song, and it's always greeted with cheers to rival their more widely known songs.

### 'Bugs' (Vedder)

In the right hands, the accordion is a beautiful instrument. As played by, say, 'Weird Al' Yankovic, it can be used to express unselfconscious joy and go-for-broke energy. But in the wrong hands, an accordion will have you begging for mercy, longing for the soothing tones of a kazoo or a vuvuzela. At its worst, an accordion can sound like insects burrowing into your ear. And thus, we have 'Bugs': my vote for the worst-ever Pearl Jam song.

The song – if it can be called that – consists of Vedder playing a two-note, two-chord accordion riff, over which he mumbles vaguely about bugs in his head. He sounds like he's suffering an affliction: his vocals are as lifeless and off-key as his playing. You could argue that it's self-deprecating humour, but it's too boring for that. A more convincing explanation is that it's an act of deliberate provocation: 'Oh, you think we're stuck-up and self-serious?/ Well get a load of this'. To try to read anything substantial into this song, is to take it more seriously than its creator did.

## 'Satan's Bed' (Gossard, Vedder)

Confusingly, this song and *not* 'Whipping', opens with the sound of a whip crack. The drums were performed by Abbruzzese's drum technician while the drummer was in hospital. The main riff is catchy, and the squeaky guitar fills add some interest. But lyrically this is a retread of 'Corduroy', only less ambivalent and more belligerent. In case you haven't picked up on it yet, Pearl Jam aren't interested in playing the commercial pop star game. Or as Vedder crudely puts it: 'I'll never suck Satan's dick'. That line is a reference to a routine by stand-up comedian Bill Hicks, in which he called advertisers 'Satan's little helpers'. Hicks was a foul-mouthed confrontational performer whose routines resembled the ranting of an apocalyptic cult leader more than they did traditional stand-up. He was resolutely anti-establishment and anti-mainstream, so it's no wonder that when he died of cancer at age 32 in February 1994 (two months before Kurt Cobain), he became another martyr for the alternative scene.

## 'Better Man' (Vedder)

Saving the best for (almost) last, here is the album's big radio hit, and one of Pearl Jam's very best songs. After a spooky opening of wailing feedback, a gentle guitar figure rings out. Again it's a short repeating figure that never fully resolves, and it generates a sense of stillness. Vedder paints an appropriate picture: a woman lying in bed, watching the clock, waiting for her husband to come home. When the chorus hits, you realise why she's so apprehensive: 'She lies and says she's in love with him'; 'She dreams in colour/She dreams in red'. Her husband is abusive.

Crucially, the full band doesn't enter on this first chorus. That would've turned the song into a kind of anthem. Instead, the band enter halfway through the second verse, after the woman has talked herself out of leaving him. 'There's no one else who needs to know', she says to herself. Like many victims of domestic abuse, she feels like it's somehow her fault, and she'll be judged for leaving him. When the band come in and the song kicks into high gear, it's as if all the frustration and fear have bubbled over. This is the emotional flip side of 'Animal'; Vedder's empathy is expressed as a cry of despair rather than rage.

Like The Police's 'Every Breath You Take' and R.E.M.'s 'The One I Love', this song is frequently misinterpreted. It's likely it became a hit because the big hook line 'Can't find a better man' sounds superficially romantic. But she isn't saying she can't find a better man because she's already found the best: she's lamenting that she's got no other option. The line that comes before should make it obvious: 'She lies and says she's in love with him'. But never underestimate the radio-listening public's capacity for missing the obvious.

Remarkably, Vedder wrote this song while he was still in high school. The band began working on it during the *Vs.* sessions, but put it aside because Brendan O'Brien thought it had the potential to be a hit. Woe be it that Pearl Jam should consciously record a hit song! Fortunately for them and us, O'Brien rescued it for this album. True to form, they didn't release it as an official single, but it still reached number 1 on the US rock chart. It's their second-most-performed non-*Ten* song, and the crowd usually sing the entire opening section before the band come in. Pearl Jam fans can take the darkest material, and turn it into a communal bonding experience.

## 'Aye Davanita' (Abbruzzese, Ament, Gossard, McCready, Vedder)

This scrap of a song is the first manifestation of Pearl Jam's art rock inclinations. The backwards drums and warped vocals provide a modest diversion for a minute. The problem is, that the song goes on for three minutes. The title – which also forms whatever lyrics aren't just vowel sounds – has no meaning as far as my research has turned up. On this song's page in the booklet, there's a short poem about a woman who thinks of herself as a work of art. Your guess is as good as mine.

## 'Immortality' (Vedder)

A gloomy, quintessentially grungy guitar figure opens the album's other ballad epic. The vibe is similar to 'Indifference', except Vedder's voice never rises above a whisper. The feeling here is of resignation rather than defiance. Lyrically, it's an impressionistic rumination on the pressures of fame ('Victims in demand for public show'), drug use ('Artificial tear, vessel stabbed') and suicide ('Some die just to live'). This has led to speculation that it's about Kurt Cobain, but Vedder denies this. He told the *L.A. Times* that any attempt to write directly about Cobain would seem exploitative, and he was correct. But you can't deny that this song describes exactly what happened to Cobain after he died: he achieved a tragic kind of immortality as a martyr to his idea of authenticity.

A terrific bluesy solo unlike anything McCready has done thus far, gives this song a back porch country-blues vibe. It feels close to home, musically and emotionally. It's the perfect ending to Pearl Jam's most personal album yet. Or at least, it would be if not for...

## 'Hey Foxymophandlemama, That's Me' (Ament, Gossard, Irons, McCready, Vedder)

The only reason I don't declare this eight-minute drone to be Pearl Jam's all-time worst song, is that it comes at the end of the album, whereas you have to actively *skip* 'Bugs'. It's unlikely that even the most committed Pearl Jam superfan would've listened to this more than once.

The underlying idea of the song is worth something. Over the desultory instrumental track, there are snippets of a TV segment that Vedder recorded when he was 17 – the words of patients let out of psychiatric care while they were still in need of help, because the government had cut funding – a worthy issue to shed light on, but this is an unworthy vehicle for it.

The song's most notable thing is that it marked the band's first appearance of their drummer for the following two albums: Jack Irons. Formerly of Red Hot Chili Peppers, Irons is the man who gave Vedder the demo cassette that changed his life. He would make his presence felt on the next album. But here, his drums sound like Nick Mason's on one of Pink Floyd's late-1960s space rock songs such as 'A Saucerful of Secrets'.

## Vitalogy (Reissue bonus tracks)

The 2011 *Vitalogy* reissue – originally combined with *Vs.*, but now available separately – comes with three bonus tracks. None of them are new songs, so I won't address them in individual entries, but they are worth hearing. There's a mix of 'Better Man' that includes only Vedder's guitar and O'Brien's organ. This version would *never* be mistaken for a romantic anthem, and it arguably gets the point of the song across more clearly. It also highlights the incredible sensitivity of Vedder's vocal performance. There's an alternate take of 'Corduroy' that has more bass noodling in the intro and more pronounced acoustic guitar in the chorus. Finally, there's a demo of 'Nothingman' which is obviously less polished but stands on its own quite well.

# Mirror Ball/Merkin Ball (1995)

Personnel:
Jeff Ament: bass
Stone Gossard, Mike McCready: guitar
Jack Irons: drums, percussion
Eddie Vedder: backing vocals, lead vocals on Merkin Ball album
Neil Young: lead vocals, guitar, pump organ
With:
Brendan O'Brien: bass on 'I Got Id'
Producers: Brendan O'Brien, Brett Eliason
Recorded at Bad Animals Studio, Seattle, Washington, January-February 1995
Release date: 7 August 1995 (Mirror Ball); 4 December 1995 (Merkin Ball)
Chart places: US: 5, UK: 4 (Mirror Ball), US: 7, UK: 25 (Merkin Ball)
Running time: 55:14 (Mirror Ball); 10:53 (Merkin Ball)

By 1995, it seemed like Pearl Jam wanted to pick a fight with everybody – the music industry, concert promoters, record critics, their fellow bands and even their own fan base. But they managed to find one friend who was as bull headed and iconoclastic as they were: Neil Young.

In Seattle, over four days during January/February 1995, Pearl Jam and Young recorded the album *Mirror Ball* together. Due to the two artists being signed to different labels, Pearl Jam were not credited on the album except as individual musicians. While they essentially served as Young's backing band – with Vedder barely present – this album is well worth hearing. The sessions also produced the Pearl Jam EP *Merkin Ball*, which is essential.

Pearl Jam supported Young on a few dates of their 1993 tour leading up to the release of *Vs*. Young often brought the band out on stage to play on his song 'Rockin' In The Free World'. At the 1993 MTV Music Awards – when Pearl Jam won for 'Jeremy' – they and Young played a ferocious medley of 'Animal' and 'Rockin' In The Free World'. It seemed as if the legendary rock-and-roll maverick was passing the torch to the youngsters ready to take up his cause.

Neil Young – following his desultory 1980s genre-hopping – was on the comeback trail in 1995. 1990's feedback-drenched *Ragged Glory* – the reunion with his legendary backing band Crazy Horse – lead critics to dub him the 'Godfather of Grunge'. Kurt Cobain quoted Young's song 'Hey Hey, My My (Into The Black)' in his suicide note, to the songwriter's horror. So Young recording an album with Pearl Jam could be seen as an attempt to take control of the narrative and ease into an elder-statesman role.

Unfortunately, *Mirror Ball* fell victim to Young's perennial problem: the need for spontaneity. Nine of the eleven songs were written during the four days it took them to record the album, and all the songs were recorded live in the studio, with little embellishment. Young loves to write and record music in frantic creative bursts, to avoid overthinking things; to capture the thrill of finding the song as you play it. When inspiration strikes, it leads to incredible albums like *Tonight's The Night*. When inspiration doesn't strike, you get *Mirror Ball*. The album feels like one long jam session that failed to catch fire. There are interesting musical and lyrical ideas, but nothing is fleshed-out enough. Pearl Jam basically function as an ersatz Crazy Horse, creating a comfortable groove for Young to solo over. Vedder barely participated, because he was having problems with a stalker who made him afraid to leave his house (See 'Lukin' on *No Code*).

But a middling Neil Young album is better than many artists' best, and *Mirror Ball* has its highlights, modest though they are. 'Song X' has a swinging rhythm and a chanting chorus that makes it sound like a heavy-metal sea shanty. It and the next song 'Act Of Love' are both about abortion. Three days before the *Mirror Ball* session began, Pearl Jam and Young played the Rock For Choice benefit concert commemorating the Roe v. Wade decision. Pearl Jam would continue to play pro-choice benefits throughout their career.

Young fans cite 'I'm The Ocean' as the album's high point, because, like most of Young's best work, it's an act of self-mythologising. As a glimpse into his psyche, it's interesting, but as a song, it's rambling and unfocussed. The groovy 1960s reverie 'Downtown' is better and was released as a single. 'Throw Your Hatred Down' also has hippie vibes, being an apocalyptic plea for peace.

The most memorable song is 'Peace and Love'. It's the album's one song in which Vedder's voice is audible, although he's mixed so far down you can barely make out what he's saying. The song's message is aided by Pearl Jam performing on it. The lyrics take the form of an exchange between the two generations: baby boomers and Gen X. Young sings about the hippie dream of peace and love, and how it fell apart. Then Vedder gives his generation's perspective on it: 'I saw the dream, I saw the wake/We shared it all, but not the take'.

The February sessions also produced the two-song EP *Merkin Ball*, which was released a few months after the parent album. It is credited to Pearl Jam, though the only members who play on it are Vedder, Ament and new boy Jack Irons. Young contributes guitar, pump organ and backing vocals, while producer Brendan O'Brien plays bass on 'I Got Id'. The title refers to a 'merkin': a pubic wig, which is a joke that apparently has no deeper meaning.

The EP was one of Pearl Jam's biggest hits, reaching 7 on the *Billboard* Hot 100. Despite that, it feels as though these songs have largely been forgotten by all but Pearl Jam completists, which is a shame.

## 'I Got Id' (Vedder)

The fans and the band refer to this song by its original title: 'I Got Shit'. Epic Records asked them to change it. It's a song of self-hatred and romantic longing. If the lyrics accurately reflect Vedder's headspace at the time, he was in a bad way indeed. He describes himself as an empty shell and a cup floating on the sea. He longs for a dream 'Where I'm not ugly'. It's one of Pearl Jam's bleakest songs. It's also evidence of the limits of spontaneity. The opening guitar hook is solid, but it doesn't lead anywhere. The verse melody is unmemorable, and the chorus isn't fully developed. As with many off-the-cuff recordings of Neil Young and Pearl Jam, with a little more effort, this could've been worked up into something great. A typically scuzzy-sounding guitar solo from Young doesn't add much, but a Neil Young guitar solo is never unwelcome.

## 'The Long Road' (Vedder)

Why 'I Got Id' was included on their greatest hits set and this beauty wasn't, is a mystery. As of writing this book, 'The Long Road' is only available on the original EP, and it deserves a wider audience. Vedder wrote it after learning of the death of a teacher who once helped him through some hard times. It's lyrically simple, but a stunningly effective expression of loss and acceptance.

Jack Irons makes his presence felt for the first time, with thunderous tribal percussion that foreshadows his influence on the band's next album. Young's earthy organ sound is exquisite, but it's Vedder's guitar chords that centre the song. They are like gentle waves rocking you back and forth, and the way the melody rises and falls with his cries of sorrow ('I have wished for so long, how I wish for you today') make it feel like you've caught the band in an unguarded moment.

Even better, is the version Vedder recorded with Pakistani singer Nusrat Fateh Ali Khan for the soundtrack of the 1995 movie *Dead Man Walking*. Khan was an early-1990s cult figure due to his collaborations with Peter Gabriel, and the albums made with ambient artist Michael Brook for Gabriel's Real World label. On this version of 'The Long Road', the drums are replaced by tabla and dholak, and the organ by a harmonium. This is the traditional setup of Khan's style of music known as qawwali: a form of devotional Islamic singing. In between Vedder's verses, Khan sings with astonishing force and fervour. He turns this song into the prayer it always was at heart.

# No Code (1996)

Personnel:
Jeff Ament: bass, backing vocals, guitar, Chapman stick
Stone Gossard: guitar, backing vocals, lead vocals on 'Mankind'
Mike McCready: guitar, piano
Eddie Vedder: lead vocals, guitar, harmonica, sitar
With:
Brendan O'Brien: piano
Producer: Brendan O'Brien
Recorded at Chicago Recording, Chicago; Kingsway, New Orleans; Studio Litho,
Seattle, July 1995-May 1996
Release date: 27 August 1996
Chart places: US: 1, UK: 3
Running time: 49:37

Around *No Code*'s release, there was a sense that for all their sales and acclaim,
Pearl Jam were on the ropes. Their protest against Ticketmaster meant they
had to curtail their last tour. They replaced their drummer for the second time,
and band members were bristling at Vedder's increased dominance. Ament
even contemplated quitting – and no wonder, since they began the recording
sessions *without* him!

In stark contrast to the recording of *Mirror Ball*, the sessions for *No Code*
were spread out over a year. The members brought in snippets of music and
worked them into songs via jamming: a time-consuming process that led to a
lot of dead ends. Vedder frequently had to wait a long time for something he
could put words to. Tempers were bound to fray. But their choice of a new
drummer was fortuitous. Jack Irons was well-liked by all, and he encouraged
the members to share their feelings. They came out the other side of the
recording process feeling a lot more positive about the band.

As for the album itself... that's a matter of opinion. These are the facts: *No
Code* was the last Pearl Jam album to top the album chart; it sold less than
half of what its predecessor did during its first week; it was their first album
to not go multiplatinum. Critical assessment was mostly in accordance: it was
considered a fragmentary, borderline-incoherent record with no flow and no
obvious singles. But the mistake critics made was in thinking of any of this as
a bad thing. Unlike on *Vitalogy*, the experiments on *No Code* almost all work.
The rockers are harder and the ballads are softer than ever before, meaning
that it never feels like the band is stuck in a rut. There are no throwaways or
sketches, and the herky-jerky sequencing means the album keeps springing
surprises. What might have seemed like directionless floundering at the time,
now seems like the smartest move they could've made to avoid being swept
into the rubbish bin of history along with so much of the *alternative* scene.

In 1996, alternative rock – like Pearl Jam – was in a seemingly constant
state of transition. After Kurt Cobain died in 1994, the media looked around

for the next 'voice of a generation'. The other grunge figureheads (Vedder, Layne Stanley, Chris Cornell, Scott Weiland) had problems of their own to deal with and did not want the same kind of scrutiny that Cobain had to endure. In any case, the grunge wave had already crested by this point, and other forms of alt-rock were gaining a foothold on the market. In 1994 alone, Nine Inch Nails released their industrial goth epic *The Downward Spiral*, which made all the other alt-rock albums of the era (including Pearl Jam's) seem quaint in comparison – Oasis debuted with the decidedly and deliberately retrograde *Definitely Maybe*, which – along with Blur's *Parklife* – defined the new 'Britpop' sound; Green Day's *Dookie* and The Offspring's *Smash* made pop punk the new sound of youth; Sunny Day Real Estate's *Diary* and Weezer's self-titled *'Blue Album'* launched the second wave of emo, which would outlast all these other genres by a decade. By 1996, the hippest names in music were the genre blenders like Beck, Bjork and Garbage, whose music mixed elements of alternative rock, pop, hip-hop, electronica and exotica. Punk-rock puritanism was out, and eclecticism was in. Pearl Jam did not try to sound like any of those other bands. That would've been disastrous. Like The Cure, U2 and R.E.M. before them, Pearl Jam added new elements to their sound without sacrificing their core identity. They changed things up just enough to outrun the zeitgeist.

Fittingly, the packaging is Pearl Jam's most elaborate and finicky. The cover consists of 144 Polaroid photos arranged in a grid. Some are of random objects, while others are distressing close-ups of body parts and wounds. When you unfold the cover and see the complete 12x12 spread, the darker parts of the photos form an Eye of Providence logo, which you can also see in the Polaroid that gives the album its title. In a medical context, the title means 'Do not resuscitate', but it could also refer to Pearl Jam's refusal to abide by any set of rules.

Each copy of *No Code* comes with a set of nine replica Polaroids. On the back of each are printed the lyrics and credits for a different song. Since you only get nine per CD, you'd have to buy duplicate copies of the album to get the whole set. Or maybe Pearl Jam envisioned fans trading their photos like kids do baseball cards. The set I own is missing 'Sometimes', 'Red Mosquito' and 'Present Tense'. I'm annoyed I don't have 'Red Mosquito' since that card features the lyrics drawn in the shape of a bug. Equally annoying is that the 'In My Tree' and 'I'm Open' cards don't include their lyrics! This was the first Pearl Jam album to credit the individual writers of every song. Presumably, this helped mitigate the feeling that Vedder was hogging the spotlight.

*No Code* sold respectably, but it didn't have the impact of Pearl Jam's first three albums. And that's okay – a fall-off was bound to happen eventually, if only due to changing tastes. What *No Code did* manage was to affirm fans' faith in the band; that they weren't alt-rock interlopers or coattail riders, but true artists who were able to evolve their sound. It turned out that Pearl Jam's fans – like the band themselves – appreciate a challenge.

## 'Sometimes' (Vedder)

Shock of shocks: this album opens not with a bang, but with a whisper. As if to prepare the listener for further surprises to come, this song starts quiet and stays quiet. Like much of the album, 'Sometimes' has a hushed late-night feel, and here that's aided by subtle thunder sound effects. The subdued arrangement gives Ament's bass, room to shine. He creates a warm cocoon of sound while Gossard and McCready (on piano) pluck soft notes out of the night sky like shooting stars. Vedder's singing gets louder and louder, but just when it threatens to get histrionic, he restrains himself. He starts with an impressionistic depiction of God as a painter, and finishes by reflecting on his own internal contradictions. It's a statement of intent for the entire album: sometimes I'm one thing, sometimes I'm another, expect the unexpected.

## 'Hail, Hail' (Ament, Gossard, McCready, Vedder)

Now this is more like it! As soon as 'Sometimes' finishes, the raspy riff of 'Hail, Hail' comes slamming in. Within a couple of bars, Jack Irons proves he can cut the mustard as a straight-down-the-line rock drummer. This made for a reassuring second single from the album, after the curveball of 'Who You Are'.

Lyrically it's a relatively straightforward internal monologue about a failing relationship – the kind where you're only sticking with it out of a sense of obligation. The 'lucky ones' that Vedder hails in the chorus, are the ones who are truly in love. There's no bitterness in his vocal though, only resignation. The music fits the theme well. Just when the song seems to be gearing up for a massive solo, it eases off the throttle. The middle eight's chiming guitars are strangely soothing, despite the storm raging all around. Vedder croons, 'I can only be as good as you'll let me': a line that encapsulates the feeling of co-dependency. He follows that with 'Are you woman enough to be my man?': an interesting line whose interpretation depends on whether you think he's singing in character or not. There's also a line in the first verse that could be the thesis statement for the entire album: 'I don't wanna think, I wanna feel'.

## 'Who You Are' (Gossard, Irons, Vedder)

Just as the frenzy of 'Hail, Hail' fades away, this song fades in like a soothing breeze. Jack Irons' multi-layered drum pattern emerges from the fog, sounding like all five of the band's hearts beating in unison, while gentle guitar strums and Vedder's electric sitar, ring in the new morning. The melody feels timeless because it's so simple; just the E and B chord, back and forth like a mother rocking her baby. Vedder's gentle melody and soulful vocal performance make it feel like a lullaby: the kind of tune you've always known. The ragged harmonies add to the song's homemade feel. This began as a drum instrumental from Irons, and the band incorporated Vedder's experience working with Nusrat Fateh Ali Khan. The end result is one of Pearl Jam's most beautiful songs.

Lyrically it's quite simple – just a series of three-to-five syllable phrases like Zen koans, about the transient nature of all things and the need to push past what's standing in your way. There's no real chorus, only variations on the title phrase. It's an impressionistic song, designed to evoke a feeling rather than be interpreted literally. The sense of release after the bridge when the snare drum enters – as Vedder sings 'Just a little time before we leave' – is one of the best moments in Pearl Jam's discography. On the *Rearviewmirror* collection, the song has slightly different lyrics: 'Circumstance, clapping hands' became 'Avalanche, falling fast'. This change was preserved on all subsequent *No Code* reissues.

When Pearl Jam released this song as *No Code*'s first single, it was a deliberate curveball. intended – so they say – to prevent their audience from growing any bigger. It's too lovely a song to be thought of as a provocation, so the response at the time was more like befuddlement. In one respect, their ploy completely failed, as this was the song that made me a Pearl Jam fan. I fell in love with this song without even knowing who it was. It was only while I waited by the radio to tape it from the hit parade that I learned it was Pearl Jam. I went right out and bought the album.

## 'In My Tree' (Gossard, Irons, Vedder)
This is another song based around a tribal drum pattern, but this one is more ominous. The sound of the drums is muted, but they're played so fast that it sounds like an oncoming storm. Irons manages to build up an incredible sense of tension in the short instruction before the rough sheets of guitar come crashing down like rain. The keyboards that sound like dollar-store pan flutes, add to the sense of panic. Thematically it's another leave-me-alone-I-don't-want-to-be-famous' song, and the music's density makes it sound like you're trapped in Vedder's head – up in his mental hideaway where the fans and critics can't hurt him. Eventually, the tribal drums give way to crashing snare, and the song gets even more frantic. When Vedder cries at the climax, 'Got back my innocence/Still got it, still got it', it sounds like he's trying to convince him*self*.

## 'Smile' (Ament, Vedder)
Working with Neil Young, no doubt rubbed off on the band, because this song feels very indebted to his despondent mid-1970s music. The highest compliment I can pay to a song as simple as 'Smile', is that it wouldn't have felt out of place on Young's *Tonight's The Night*. The lyrics come from a note (reproduced on the lyric card) that Dennis Flemion of The Frogs slipped to Vedder. Flemion asks repeatedly, 'Don't it make you smile?', to which the answer is, not really. This is a downer of a song, based around a loping minor-key riff that sounds as if the band just rolled out of bed and started playing. Adding to the doleful feel is some bleating harmonica from Vedder, and a couple of brief guitar solos that are distorted to Dinosaur Jr. levels of ear-

bleeding. Despite all that, this is a likeable song. The chorus cry of 'I miss you always' sounds utterly sincere and guileless.

### 'Off He Goes' (Vedder)

The final song on side one of a vinyl record is something of a hallowed position. It's where artists often hide their best long-form songs; the kind of intimate epics that make fans feel like they've discovered something. Famous side-one final tracks include The Who's 'The Song Is Over', Bruce Springsteen's 'Backstreets', Billy Joel's 'Scenes From An Italian Restaurant', and of course – the granddaddy of them all – Led Zeppelin's 'Stairway To Heaven'.

Unlike those songs, 'Off He Goes *was* released as a single. But it barely charted anywhere, and it's only just in their top-50 most-played live songs. This is an injustice because it's the equal to those aforementioned songs. From the tasteful acoustic riff to the elegant chords, to the indelible melody, to the warm production, the song's individual components combine to make magic.

The song is about that classic rock-and-roll archetype, the wanderer. Just like the Dion song, this is about a man who can't be tied down. Whether he's driven by demons or self-doubt or some kind of innate need, he's always on the move. Vedder sings from the perspective of one of the people left behind. He wonders if the man can be fixed, or if he even needs fixing, because when he returns, it's as if nothing has changed. But the cycle repeats. Compared to the grim 'Nothingman' and 'Immortality', this is more sympathetic to its subject. That makes sense, as Vedder told *Spin* that this is partly a self-portrait, though the fact that he sings it in third-person means he was keeping some distance between the song and himself.

### 'Habit' (Vedder)

A furious punk song with a rubbery-sounding riff. Nothing new musically, but it's a terrific example of Pearl Jam's musical syncopation. This is the band's bluntest antidrug song yet. Vedder sings in a truly scary guttural tone to let us know how much he means what he says. That said, 80% of the lyrics are just the line 'Never thought you'd habit' repeated over and over. The 'you' in question is Mike McCready. During the making of *Vitalogy*, the guitarist had sought treatment for drug and alcohol abuse, and was clean by 1995. His sobriety would not last, but he is clean now.

### 'Red Mosquito' (Ament, Gossard, Irons, McCready, Vedder)

This song has a similar feel to 'Deep', though it's more of a proper song and less of a self-indulgent excuse for soloing. But what a fantastic solo we get! McCready's guitar tone is high and thin with a 'stinging' quality that suits the song's themes. This is arguably the most unabashedly 1970s-sounding the band would ever get, what with launching straight into the solo, and the lyrics borrowing an old blues motif. This is a classic Satan's-coming-for-you song, following the template Robert Johnson laid down in 1937 with 'Hell Hound On My Trail'.

**Above:** Pearl Jam in 1993, with Eddie Vedder glaring as if you've just called his band 'the new Mötley Crüe'.

**Below:** ... and in 2018: an older, wiser, more contented band.

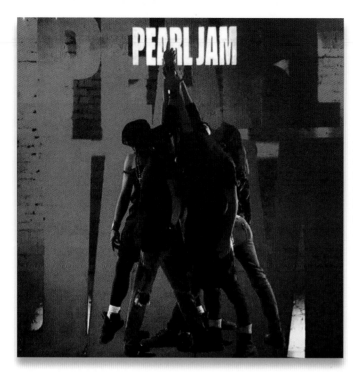

**Left:** All for one! The cover of *Ten* evokes the camaraderie that would carry the band through their tumultuous career. (*Epic*)

**Right:** *Singles:* possibly the largest ever disparity between the quality of a movie and quality of its soundtrack. (*Epic*)

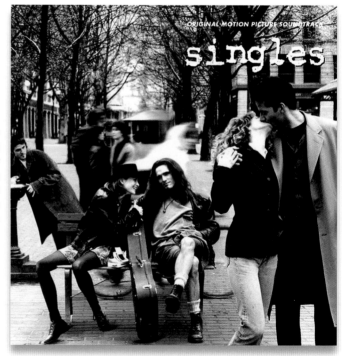

**Right:** Wake up sheeple! It's Pearl Jam *Vs.* the world on their hard-hitting sophomore album. (*Epic*)

**Left:** *Vitalogy*, or the art of making difficult but compelling third albums. (*Epic*)

**Left:** Google 'archetypal grunge song' and they'll likely show you this promo clip for 'Even Flow'.

**Right:** You can see why Time magazine titled their article about Eddie Vedder 'All the Rage'.

**Left:** Stone Gossard ripping through 'Even Flow'.

**Right:** Dave Abbruzzese. After all these years, he's still many fan's preferred Pearl Jam drummer.

**Left:** Mike McCready, lost in his work.

**Right:** The 'Even Flow' video – Pearl Jam building a connection with fans who would stick with them through thick and thin.

**Left:** Neil Young's *Mirror Ball* – Reprise Records must have been livid that they weren't allowed to credit Pearl Jam on the cover. (*Reprise*)

**Right:** *Merkin Ball* – technically Pearl Jam's highest-charting original song, depending on how you define a 'single'.

**Left:** On their fourth album, Pearl Jam declared they had *No Code*, and they could have had no sales. (*Epic*)

**Right:** Forget which drummer you prefer, the real question is do you prefer Eddie with long or short hair?

**Left:** Matt Cameron joining on drums gave Pearl Jam the stability they needed to survive.

**Right:** Performing 'I Am Mine' on the Late Show with David Letterman in 2002.

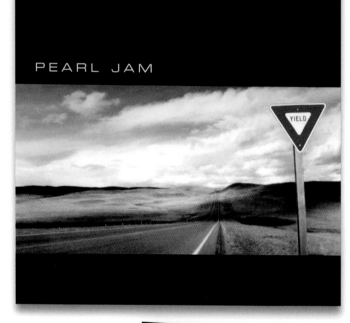

**Left:** *Yield* to the subtle charms of Pearl Jam's underrated fifth album.

**Right:** Pearl Jam's rootsy music contrasts with the cosmic cover art of their fifth album *Binaural*. *(Epic)*

**Right:** After the tragedy at Roskilde, Pearl Jam returned to read people the *Riot Act*. (*Epic*)

**Left:** *Lost Dogs* – Pearl Jam's rarities collection – is way better than the trash can on the cover would have you believe! (*Epic*)

**Left:** Best foot forward – it's Pearl Jam's *Greatest Hits*! (*Epic*)

**Right:** They can't all be winners. Pearl Jam's hard-rocking self-titled album has their most incongruous artwork. (*J*)

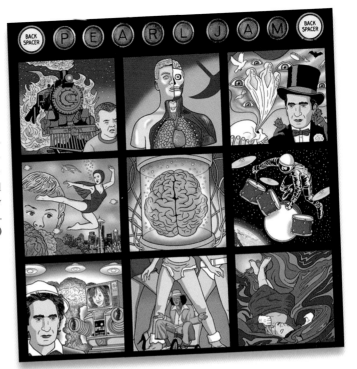

**Right:** *Backspacer* – wild cover art for a straightforwardly commercial and relatively mellow album. (*Monkeywrench*)

**Left:** *Pearl Jam Twenty*, the band's Cameron Crowe-directed victory lap. (*Columbia*)

**Left:** By 2009, the man responsible for the howling rage of 'Animal' was now writing mellow tunes like 'Just Breathe'.

**Right:** You know you've hit the big time when you can afford to hire a string quartet for your concert.

**Left:** ELP eat your heart out! The lovely 'The End' gets a boost from live strings.

**Right:** *Lightning Bolt*: an album cover that looks like the logo for a Pearl Jam brand energy drink. (*Monkeywrench*)

**Left:** On *Gigaton*, they chose some epic album art that reflected the scope of the music within. (*Monkeywrench*)

**Left:** Buona sera! It's Pearl Jam live in Rome in 2018.

**Right:** Mike McCready getting mellow in 2018.

**Left:** Eddie Vedder, perhaps calling out the lone fan who's demanding to hear 'Bugs' live.

**Right:** After twenty-plus years, Pearl Jam would simply not feel the same without Matt Cameron on the drums.

**Left:** Stone Gossard in 2018, still rockin' hard!

**Right:** Jeff Ament – from the beginning, the bassist was Pearl Jam's secret weapon.

**Left:** *Live on Two Legs* – the first, and perhaps least, of Pearl Jam's many, *many* live albums. (*Epic*)

**Right:** The semi-acoustic *Live at Benaroya Hall* – a fine complement to the *Unplugged* session from a decade earlier. (*BMG*)

**Left:** *Temple Of The Dog* - thirty years later, we shouldn't forget where it all began. (*A&M*)

One of the unintended consequences of punk's crusade to escape the shadow of 1970s blues rock, was that it also lost touch with rock and roll's roots in God-fearing gospel. The red mosquito 'must have been the Devil', says Vedder, and its bite is a warning that the horned one lies in wait for us all. So you could consider this song to be Pearl Jam's equivalent of Van Halen's 'Runnin' With The Devil'. From *No Code* onwards, Pearl Jam would seem more conformable citing well-worn classic rock tropes. As Vedder sings, 'If I had known then what I know now'.

## 'Lukin' (Vedder)

Like too many celebrities, Eddie Vedder has been the victim of a stalker. This song tells of when a woman with mental problems believed that Pearl Jam's songs were about her, and that Vedder was the father of her children. She drove her car into Vedder's house and almost killed herself. Vedder then installed new fences and hired 24-hour security to protect himself and his wife. When people sneer at celebrities who complain about their problems, they forget about situations like this.

This song is only a minute long, and it sounds absolutely furious. Vedder barks out the lyrics on the beat, one syllable at a time. He doesn't go into detail, but he mentions the paternity issue, and the chilling final line is, 'The last I heard, that freak was purchasing a fucking gun'. The title refers to Matt Lukin: then bassist of Mudhoney. He had nothing to do with the stalker; his house is referred to as a place of safety.

## 'Present Tense' (McCready, Vedder)

This song opens with gentle chiming guitar sounds, similar to The Edge's work on U2's 'The Unforgettable Fire'. Vedder muses on the meaning of life, and asks us if we've given the matter enough thought. When the chorus hits, thick stabs of bass seem to poke at the listener, as if to say 'Pay attention, I have an answer'.

> You can spend your time alone
> Re-digesting past regrets
> Or you can come to terms and realise
> You're the only one who can't forgive yourself
> Makes much more sense to live in the present tense

After the second chorus, a fast one-note guitar figure enters: again, very U2-ish. Then the whole band joins in and the song shoots off into the stratosphere as if they were chasing the mysterious light that Vedder sings about. It's this uplifting climax that makes this song a concert favourite. This is the album's third-most-performed song; played far more than any of the singles other than 'Hail Hail'. You have to have total command over your audience for a song like this to work live. You have to keep them spellbound and silent for the first half, so the explosion at the end works as a payoff.

## 'Mankind' (Gossard)

This was the first Pearl Jam song without Vedder on lead vocals, and the only such included on an album. The song doesn't gain anything from being sung by Gossard. His adenoidal voice makes this sound more like the work of Urge Overkill or Blind Melon; great bands to sound like, but coming after 'Present Tense', it kind of breaks the spell. It's a pop song about the insincere nature of facile pop songs, and Gossard wrote it just to see if he could. He could've saved the band the trouble and just covered R.E.M.'s 'Pop Song 89' instead.

## 'I'm Open' (Irons, Vedder)

Over a bed of ambient noise that sounds electronic even if it isn't, Vedder softly recites a short poem reflecting on childhood and lost innocence. The line 'He decides to dream, dream up a new self for himself', cuts to the heart of every child who's ever longed to reinvent themselves: often as a rock star.

This is a good song with which to gauge people's opinion of Pearl Jam, and of rock poetry in general. For some, it's an embarrassingly pretentious piece of pseudo-intellectual codswallop in the tradition of Jim Morrison at his most self-indulgent. For others, it's a beautifully pretentious piece of pseudo-intellectual codswallop in the tradition of Jim Morrison at his most self-indulgent.

## 'Around The Bend' (Vedder)

Now we're back in Neil Young territory, but this time it's circa *Harvest*. Bent strings and honky-tonk piano (played by O'Brien) create a warm relaxing-on-the-back-porch feel. The album ends not on a note of bile or regret, but of looking forward to better days just out of sight. It ends suddenly as if the band arrived at their destination sooner than expected.

# Yield (1998)

Personnel:
Jeff Ament: bass, backing vocals
Stone Gossard: guitar, backing vocals
Jack Irons: drums, percussion, vocals
Mike McCready: lead guitar
Eddie Vedder: lead vocals, rhythm guitar
Producer: Brendan O'Brien
Recorded at Doppler and Southern Tracks Recording, Atlanta; Studio Litho and Bad Animals, Seattle, February-September 1997
Release date: 3 February 1998
Chart places: US: 2, UK: 7
Running time: 48:37

By 1998, grunge was done and dusted. Soundgarden and Screaming Trees had broken up, and Alice in Chains were in limbo as their singer Layne Stanley sank into drug addiction. Mudhoney were the last men flying the flag for the original Seattle sound, and they were happier being an underground band. Beyond Seattle, Billy Corgan had fired the drummer from Smashing Pumpkins, and adopted a more electronic approach. Soon he would fire the rest of the band too. The original lineups of The Breeders, L7 and Veruca Salt were also done. Stone Temple Pilots were hanging on, but just barely. The stories were almost all the same – a combination of drugs, ego and media pressure undermined their camaraderie and creativity. 'Tis a tale as old as rock.

Grunge's decline was reflected in the wider alternative culture. Flannel shirts and ripped jeans were out; sportswear and baggy low-riding pants were in. Floppy hair and scruffy beards were replaced by frosted tips and dyed goatees. It was pop punk acts like Green Day, The Offspring and No Doubt (irreverent, energetic, fun-loving) that embodied the zeitgeist now. Beyond that, mainstream culture shifted away from dressing down and trying to be *authentic*. Now, conspicuous consumption and personal branding was *in*. The era of shiny-suit hip hop embodied by artists like Puff Daddy and (early) Jay-Z, was upon us. Soon, rap would overtake alt-rock as the way for youth to rebel against their parents' ideas of decorum and *real music*.

It was into this unforgiving environment that Pearl Jam released *Yield*: their greatest album that isn't *Ten* or *Vs.*. While *Yield* predictably failed to match the success of their earlier albums, over time it has become one of their most acclaimed releases. Every great artist has that one album that's not a huge critical or commercial success, but which is claimed by the fan collective as their special favourite. This is usually an album perched between what made the artist great to begin with and what they were capable of, going forward. Think The Beatles' *Let It Be;* think Bruce Springsteen's *Darkness On The Edge Of Town;* think R.E.M.'s *Document*. Like those did for their artists, *Yield* embodies the spirit of Pearl Jam better than many of their more-acclaimed releases.

*Yield* was Pearl Jam's most experimental effort thus far. But paradoxically it also showcased their roots rock side, with elements of folk, blues, and country now incorporated into their basic sound instead of highlighted on specific tracks. In reaching for a more sunny, open and optimistic sound, the band managed to align themselves with where mainstream rock was at in the mid-to-late-1990s. Around 1994, a range of acts emerged who were nominally *alternative*, but more overtly populist in the style of Bruce Springsteen and Tom Petty.

These were bands that sounded more as if they used 'Daughter' as a template instead of 'Alive': catchy but serious-minded songs with elements of dark Americana to them. Live were one of the first, with their hits 'I Alone' and 'Lightning Crashes'. Soul Asylum (who actually predate Pearl Jam) broke through with 'Runaway Train': a folk rock ditty about missing children. Matchbox 20 had the hit 'Push': about female-on-male domestic abuse. Hootie & The Blowfish had a name to make critics chuckle, but the laughter ceased when the band outsold every critically acclaimed alternative artist with their grunged-down bar-band rock. Their hit song 'Let Her Cry' was self-serious enough to make Vedder seem like Primus' Les Claypool. These bands were a thread connecting alt-rock back to the iconic singer-songwriters of the post-Woodstock era. Hootie's 'Only Wanna Be with You' and Counting Crows' 'Mr. Jones' both made explicit reference to Bob Dylan. Save for Hootie's Darius Rucker – whose sonorous vocals were often a dead ringer for Vedder at his most marble-mouthed – none of these bands sounded that much like Pearl Jam. Mostly they sounded like R.E.M. without the mystique. But as far as radio programmers were concerned, the bands were tailor-made for the audience who made 'Better Man' a hit but were turned off by songs like 'Spin The Black Circle' and 'Who You Are'. By 1998, there was no doubt that in American rock, anger and abrasion were out, and empathic storytelling was in.

It's not as if Pearl Jam made a conscious effort to reestablish their preeminence amongst these new bands. By this point, they were secure enough to do what they wanted. But *Yield* feels like they finally shook off all expectations associated with being a Seattle band, and felt free to explore other sounds in a relaxed and organic way. Compared to *Vitalogy* and *No Code*, none of the *Yield* experiments and tangents feel forced or intrusive. *Yield* creates its own internal world of promises and possibilities, and over the course of a listen, it fulfils that sense of longing, in the vein of albums like Springsteen's *Born to Run* and Tom Petty and the Heartbreakers' *Damn The Torpedoes*.

The cover art and booklet are appealing and engrossing. The front cover image of a Montana highway stretching off into the distance is classic American road-trip imagery, evoking the feeling of freedom and adventure that the music generates. When you open the cover, a triangle cut-out reveals that the 'Yield' sign is now sticking out of the ocean: a neat visual pun. Inside the booklet, the lyrics for each song are typed and legible for once, but still mostly incomplete. Each song is accompanied by an evocative black-and-white photo: most of them by Ament. As a whole, the package adds to the album's widescreen.

*Yield* was released while the *Titanic* soundtrack ruled the charts with an iron fist, so Pearl Jam missed hitting the top spot in the US for the first time since *Ten*. In the long run though, *Yield* outsold its predecessor. This was partly because Pearl Jam abandoned their fight against Ticketmaster, and finally underwent a full North American tour. They followed this with more international tours, and the album reliably hit the top 10 around the world.

## 'Brain Of J' (McCready, Vedder)

After a hurried count-in and a false start, the band slam into this crude but rousing punk song. 'Who's got the brain of JFK/What's it mean to us now?', asks Vedder. As we know from the movie, they saved Hitler's brain, so why not Kennedy's? This song seems to be about the desire for a leader with the charisma and vision of past heroes. The way Vedder's voice catches during the chorus, adds an element of desperation to the song. 'The whole world will be different soon/The whole world will be relieved'. He sounds like he's trying to convince him*self*.

As far as Pearl Jam album openers go, this is probably in the bottom half. But after the experiments of *No Code*, it establishes that the band is ready to rock. But the relatively quiet melodic instrumental middle eight suggests that they still have some tricks up their sleeves.

## 'Faithful' (McCready, Vedder)

A burst of distortion abruptly gives way to this song, which is about as far from the opener as it could get. Gentle drumming and lush waves of guitar create a serene mood. Vedder enters with a casual vocal style not far removed from a talking blues. His lyrics are a standard agnostic litany; a series of half-formed thoughts evoking a general air of scepticism towards the idea of a higher power: 'Who's upstairs?', 'Belief in a game', 'M.Y.T.H.' etc. The music builds steadily to the chorus, which cuts in as Vedder declares, 'I'm through with screaming'. And indeed, this song benefits from his restraint. It's to Vedder's credit that he doesn't snarl and growl his way through this anti-religion song. Instead, he sounds confident. While everyone else is faithful to this imaginary man in the sky, Vedder promises that he'll be faithful to one special person: be it his wife or the person listening. The crisp production and dynamic playing, evoke the feel of the wide-open sky, which is perfect for a song about spirituality.

## 'No Way' (Gossard)

This song is a first for Pearl Jam: Vedder singing lyrics that he didn't write. Thematically, it's something he *could've* written – expressing mental uncertainty and the hope that someone might intervene and help. But it differs from his lyric style in two ways. For one thing, the verses are filled with internal rhymes and double meanings, which adds an element of playfulness to an otherwise gloomy song. For another, it climaxes with the somewhat fatalistic cry of 'I'll stop trying to make a difference': a very un-Vedder-like sentiment. It's the music that makes this song. It's driven by a raspy rhythmic riff and a stomping Zeppelin-esque rhythm, and it builds relentlessly with layers of feedback and wah-wah. The bass entry on the second verse is especially cool.

## 'Given To Fly' (McCready, Vedder)

This is indisputably one of Pearl Jam's top-five songs, and I would go as far as to call it their greatest song released as a single. It embodies aspects of the band that songs like 'Alive' do not – their unabashed ambition, their openhearted inclusivity, and their forever-questing sensibility.

'Given To Fly' began with the guitar figure composed by McCready. It's a thing of simple beauty; a sound that's simultaneously liquid and crystalline. Some noted its superficial similarity to the acoustic riff of Led Zeppelin's 'Going To California'. That song is a pastoral reverie that functions as an interlude amidst the *sturm und drang* of *Led Zeppelin IV*, whereas McCready's 'Given To Fly' riff serves as a launchpad for a full-on flight of fancy.

Vedder sings of a man who is feeling disconnected from society; who runs until he comes to the ocean, where he takes flight. He returns to share what he's learned, and is attacked for it. But he stands tall and sends his love regardless. It's easy to read this song as autobiographical – the reference to waves delivering him wings could refer to Vedder's love of surfing, and the men who strip and stab him could be read as critics or stalkers. But the lyrics have more of an allegorical feel. Vedder told the *Philadelphia Inquirer* that he envisioned the song as a children's picture book. It's the perennial story of the Messianic figure who transcends society's constraints and is rejected for it. The Who's *Tommy* is another classic example.

Whatever the intended meaning, the song captures the joy of living in the moment, or leaving your troubles behind for just a little while. It's one of the band's greatest ensemble performances. Irons' nimble drumming propels the song along while also giving it a weightless feel. Then when the band slam in and Vedder opens his voice all the way up, it's spine-tingling.

This was rightly released as the album's first single. It topped the US rock radio chart and reached the top 20 on many mainstream charts around the world, including Canada and Australia. If there was any justice in the world, it would've topped the pop charts everywhere, but in 1998, the music industry was past the point where it would allow something like that to happen. Corporations like Clear Channel were in the process of buying up local radio stations in the US, and moneymen in big cities began setting the playlists for the entire nation – ensuring that only the safest, blandest music reached a wide audience.

## 'Wishlist' (Vedder)

This is one of Vedder's calmest and most affecting songs; a far cry from the anger and bitterness of previous albums. It consists of only three chords and is based around a chugging guitar rhythm that's so simple it's almost pointillist. Not a single element of this track feels intrusive or aggravated. Even the guitar solo glides smoothly past your ears. The lyrics are indeed a wish list of metaphorical things that Vedder would like to be – a sailor who was missed; a messenger with good news; the star on top of a Christmas tree. The overall gist is that Vedder would like to be someone that another person relies on. Despite this theme of longing, the sedate pace and his measured delivery make him sound more content than ever. The only hint of bottled frustration is the opening line – 'I wish I was a neutron bomb, for one I could go off' – as if he's been the model of emotional stability up to this point. The key line is in the middle: 'I wish I was as fortunate as me'. It's as if Vedder is finally seeing the funny side of his rock star status. This was released as the second single from the album, and was a moderate hit.

## 'Pilate' (Ament)

This is the first Pearl Jam song credited solely to Jeff Ament, and it's not what anyone would've expected. One would expect some bass-driven monster rock track in the vein of early-Pearl Jam before Vedder asserted himself. This is decidedly not that. Musically it utilises the classic grunge quiet-verse/loud-chorus trick. But the lyrics are far from typical grunge fare. The verses consist of abstract lines about drawing circles, while the chorus seems completely disconnected. 'Like Pilate, I have a dog' Vedder hollers, while the backing vocals murmur, 'Obeys, kisses, misses, loves'. It's quite disconcerting, closer to Eno-esque art rock than alt-rock. According to a *Guitar World* interview, it's based on a dream Ament had after reading a Mikhail Bulgakov book, and is about the feeling of being alone. It's a catchy tune though, and its oddness helps this album seem like more than the sum of its parts.

## 'Do The Evolution' (Gossard, Vedder)

Pearl Jam have hard rockers with more-memorable riffs and catchier choruses, but none of them packs as many kick-ass ideas into under four minutes as this song does. It kicks off with a snarling stop/start riff that's almost danceable in a drunken kind of way. The band lock into a loose-but-tight groove that's reminiscent of The Stooges. This is one of the band's best arrangements and one of O'Brien's best productions. Every element asserts itself without crowding anything else out (although Ament doesn't appear on the track, and Gossard plays the bass instead). Halfway through, the riff inverts itself and takes on a snake-charming quality. Then, just when you think the track can't get any more intense, the main riff slams back in with double the force.

Vedder delivers some of his very best lyrics – a series of non-sequiturs that draw connections between the unceasing and unpitying forward-march of evolution and the equally unceasing and unpitying forced march of modern capitalism. They're framed as a series of boasts from a Patrick Bateman-type alpha male whose boasts reveal the demented selfishness underpinning the military-industrial-entertainment complex. If that sounds a little too Unabomber-ish for you, rest assured that it's all done with tongue firmly in cheek. Proof of that is the band's hilariously off-key backing vocals during the bridge: they sing 'hallelujah' like a choirboy whose voice is just breaking. Vedder also goes above and beyond with his delivery, whopping and yowling and growling and generally carrying on like a demented court jester. The lyrics were inspired by Daniel Quinn's 1992 philosophical revisionist novel *Ishmael*.

This song was not released as an official single, but it *was* the first Pearl Jam song since 'Oceans' to have a video. And what a video! It's an animation co-directed by Kevin Altieri (who directed episodes of *Batman: The Animated Series*) and Seth McFarlane (the artist/writer behind *Spawn*: one of the indie comic sensations of the 1990s). The video's producer Joe Pearson and Vedder both had input into the visuals. The video is a barrage of images that complement the lyrics literally or metaphorically. It includes just about every image that haunts our collective consciousness: concentration camps, book-burnings, battlefields and villages being bombed. It's almost too fast to follow, but it gets its power from juxtaposing one image against another. For instance, we see cavemen dancing around a fire, changing suddenly into KKK members dancing around a burning cross. There's also some dystopian predictions – like a baby being stamped with a barcode, and a man acting out a sexual assault in virtual reality. There's a recurring figure throughout – a sexy goth girl resembling Death from Neil Gaiman's *Sandman* comics. She winks at the audience and then reveals a skull for a face. One could take any frame of this video and write a doctoral thesis on its symbolic meaning. But in the end, the video's ultimate message as far as Pearl Jam is concerned, was *'Oh, you thought we didn't do videos because we couldn't make a good one? Well check this out!'*.

## '•' (red dot)' (Irons)

This song has no official name. It's represented on the back cover by an actual red dot. It's a percussion instrumental from Jack Irons. But wait, come back! This is not some self-indulgent John Bonham-style endurance test. It's only a minute long, and it's quirky and playful rather than show offish. It rolls along energetically before ending in an unintelligible childlike chant. The layers of rhythm and exotic percussion sound close to Afrobeat. This track makes you wonder how much further Irons might've pushed Pearl Jam's sound if he had stuck around after this album.

## 'MFC' (Vedder)

The title stands for 'Mini Fast Car', and this is indeed a short and fast song, perfectly evoking the feeling of hitting the road, with a sense of urgency. Vedder's lyric tells of a woman who set out on her own and disappeared. Maybe this is a happy ending for the subject of 'Better Man' (?).

Musically it's reminiscent of The Replacements' mid-1980s albums *Let It Be* and *Tim*: the highest of compliments. The main riff is very distorted, but not in a way that evokes anger. Instead, it evokes a homey warmth and wistfulness. There are also backwards guitars layered over the song, and as that was a trick most popular in the psychedelic 1960s, its use adds a sense of stepping outside of the present time.

### 'Low Light' (Ament)

The second song with words and music by Ament, is as far away from 'Pilate' as one could get. This is a lush folk song driven by acoustic guitars, with piano and keyboards adding extra warmth. This is the closest this album gets to Pearl Jam sounding like Counting Crows, Hootie & The Blowfish and all the other bands Pearl Jam set the table for – which means that ultimately this sounds like R.E.M. circa 1991/1992. What makes this song stand out from the host of imitators, is that it alternates between 6/8 and 7/8 time without a clear pattern. Ament brings the weirdness, even on such a rootsy song. According to the *Guitar World* interview, this song is the positive flip side of 'Pilate', about finding a sense of serenity within yourself.

### 'In Hiding' (Gossard, Vedder)

An interesting case, this. While 'In Hiding' was never released as a single, it managed to reach the top 20 in the US rock radio charts. It immediately became a fan favourite and an in-demand live song. And yet, I've never quite fallen under its spell. It's a terrific song, no doubt, but for me, it never lives up to the promise of Gossard's incredible opening riff. I also think the chord change going into the bridge – from D to A – robs the song of some of its momentum, and that means the chorus doesn't hit as hard as it should. It also fades out quickly after the second chorus, when a nice guitar solo would've really hit the spot.

I can still understand why many fans love this song. It's an archetypal Pearl Jam quasi-anthem that gets its emotional kick from the contrast between the music's power of and the lyric's introspective nature. Vedder was inspired by poet/writer Charles Bukowski, who would often lock himself away for days without seeing anyone. Only Pearl Jam could write a song that would get the whole crowd singing together about the need to be alone!

### 'Push Me, Pull Me' (Ament, Vedder)

This song was Pearl Jam's boldest experiment to date, and I would argue it remains one of their most successful. Amidst a swirl of feedback, effects and a sample of one of their own songs ('Happy When I'm Crying', from the 1997 fan club single), Irons lays down a stomping industrial drum track, the guitarists riff wildly whether or not they're in time, and Ament's bass lines resembles an early-1990s Madchester indie-dance band à la The Stone Roses. Vedder speaks the lyric in a sardonic drawl that makes the forced quirkiness easy to bear. This song compares favourably to the more experimental tracks from Tom Waits' *Mule Variations*. Oh, for a collaboration between those two artists!

## 'All Those Yesterdays' (Gossard)

This is the perfect closer for this album, and it may be their second-best closer after 'Release'. The music and lyrics are by Gossard, but it's far more optimistic than 'No Way'. That song climaxed with the line 'I'll stop trying to make a difference', while this song has a more helpful message about not letting your past drag you down. The line 'What are you running from, taking pills to get along?', feels like it could be directed at any number of people who were caught up in drug use in and around the band. But the chorus has a message that anybody could benefit from: 'Let them wash away, all those yesterdays'. The song builds from a simple guitar arpeggio to a big sing-along climax, with judicious use of horns adding a slight music-hall flavour that borders on sarcastic. Vedder delivers the lyric straight and sympathetic, which is ultimately what makes the song work.

## 'Hummus' (Ament, Gossard, Irons, McCready, Vedder)

This is an unlisted and uncredited two-minute track tacked onto the end: the band's first hidden track since 'Master/Slave' on *Ten*. It's a short instrumental stuck halfway between a Middle Eastern and flamenco sound.

# Binaural (2000)

Personnel:
Jeff Ament: bass
Matt Cameron: drums
Stone Gossard: rhythm guitar
Mike McCready: lead guitar
Eddie Vedder: vocals, rhythm guitar, ukulele
With:
Mitchell Froom: keyboards, harmonium
April Cameron: viola
Justine Foy: cello
Wendy Melvoin, Pete Thomas: percussion
Producer: Tchad Blake
Recorded at Studio Litho, Seattle, Washington, September 1999-January 2000
Release date: 16 May 2000
Chart places: US: 2, UK: 5
Running time: 52:05

The Yield tour – Pearl Jam's first full tour of North America in four years – was a massive success, abetted by a most improbable turn of events: namely that for a hot minute, Pearl Jam were bona fide pop stars. Their 1998 Christmas single – a cover of Wayne Cochran's 1961 teen tragedy song 'Last Kiss' – was re-released to raise money for Kosovo War refugees, and it reached number 2 on the *Billboard* Hot 100. This was something of a Pyrrhic victory, given that the song was a cover. Pearl Jam's hardcore faithful have certainly never warmed to it. But a hit is a hit, and it brought renewed attention to the band from fair-weather fans who'd drifted away. (See *Lost Dogs* for a full entry on the song.)

'Last Kiss' also introduced the public to Pearl Jam's fourth – and so far, final – drummer. Or rather, he was reintroduced, for it was Matt Cameron: erstwhile Temple Of The Dog alumnus. Cameron was fresh out of the disbanded Soundgarden, and he replaced Jack Irons between the South Pacific and North American legs of the Yield tour. Irons was unable to keep up the energy level needed for Pearl Jam's lengthy shows. Cameron was an ideal replacement, as he was simpatico with the band, and he also brought his own unique style and songwriting chops. Fans still debate who Pearl Jam's best drummer was, but almost everyone agrees that Cameron was a good choice for the sake of the band's longevity.

'Last Kiss' was an anomaly, not only in terms of Pearl Jam's career, but in terms of the wider cultural zeitgeist of the time, because in between *Yield* and *Binaural*, the next major wave of American rock music crashed into the charts and smothered them. Mainstream metal was all but dead in the 1990s, with grunge having taken its place as the heavy music *du jour*. But bubbling up from the underground, came a new form of metal, dubbed – with an unfortunate lack of imagination – nu metal. In the waning years of the 20th century, this genre overtook grunge as the young misanthrope's music of choice. Korn's 1994 debut album defined the nu metal sound: down-tuned guitars, thick distorted bass riffs, funk-influenced drumming, and cartoonish over-the-top vocals. Bands such as Sepultura, Deftones and Coal Chamber codified the sound, before Slipknot, Linkin Park and Limp Bizkit brought it into the mainstream. These last three bands put the 'nu' in 'nu metal' by incorporating hip hop elements: rapping, sampling and turntable scratching. Thus they combined the two genres of music that parents feared the most – metal and rap – ensuring that nu metal burned up fast and explosively.

This context is important in order to understand how Pearl Jam weathered the changing times. Nu metal is one of the dividing lines between Gen X and the millennials. For Gen-Xers, it represented the final fall of the alternative nation and the reassertion of style over substance. For millennials, nu metal was the sound of their childhood, and deserves as much respect as any youth movement. They are both right. Nu metal was as era-defining and impactful as grunge was – it's just that nobody wanted to admit it at the time. If you were a fan of earnest thoughtful rock music with its roots going back to the giants of the 1960s and 1970s, the advent of nu metal seemed like the apocalypse. While some of these bands have seen their critical standing rise over the last decade as they and their fandoms have endured, few would disagree that much late-1990s nu metal was facile and gimmicky. Korn's debut album shared with grunge an introspective lyric style that confronted social issues like homophobia and child abuse. But by 1998, they were rapping the 'F' slur and naming a song 'Big Black Kock'. Hit singles like Limp Bizkit's 'Nookie' and Linkin Park's 'One Step Closer' were streams of invective directed at women. When you compare the relatively convivial atmosphere of the Woodstock '94 festival to Woodstock '99 – where Limp Bizkit sung 'Give me something to break' while attendees wrecked the joint and women were sexually assaulted – it's clear that around 1999, mainstream rock turned *ugly*. And if you didn't like nu metal? Well, your other options were juvenile pop punk like Blink-182, or depressing *post-grunge* bands like Creed and Nickelback, whose baritone singers cribbed a lot of their style from Vedder, but had none of his wit and self-awareness.

Wisely, Pearl Jam chose to not compete with their chart successors. They had nothing left to prove at this point, or so they thought. To their detriment, they retreated so far into their insular world that they lost some of the verve and vigour that made them so popular to begin with. *Binaural* is not a bad album by any measure, but it is Pearl Jam's least-inviting album. It has its fans, as do all Pearl Jam albums, but it's probably the last one you'd choose to introduce someone to the band. For one thing, all the good songs are clustered in the middle, making for an unsatisfying end-to-end listening experience. This is the kind of album that mixtapes or streaming playlists were invented for.

*Binaural*'s indecisive quality can be explained by a variety of factors. McCready relapsed back into substance abuse; the band had to get used to working with Matt Cameron; Vedder suffered from writer's block and had to forgo writing music to focus on lyrics. The biggest factor was the band working with a producer other than Brendan O'Brien for the first time since *Ten*. Tchad Blake was an interesting choice, as he was best-known in 2000 for producing albums by singer-songwriters such as Elvis Costello, Neil Finn and Sheryl Crow, that saw them move away from a middle-of-the-road sound into a more experimental and abrasive realm. He utilised the binaural recording technique, which involves using two microphones placed in the positions of human ears to record the music, so it gives the listener a sense of being in the room with the musicians. This technique was used on the songs 'Nothing as It Seems', 'Off The Girl', 'Rival, 'Sleight Of Hand' and 'Soon Forget'. To experience this, you need to listen to the album with good quality headphones. Mostly, the album just sounds muddled, with the instruments separated too far apart and nothing in the centre of the mix to give it some oomph. Blake's technique also gave the album its name, and the way his recordings emphasise space and atmosphere, inspired the album art, which consists of photos of various planetary nebulae.

When *Binaural* was released, it reached the top 10 in all the usual markets (reaching number 1 in Australia and New Zealand). However, it became Pearl Jam's first album to not go platinum in the US. We could chalk this up to the changing times and the dominance of nu metal and pop punk. But in truth, this album didn't put up much of a fight. But the legacy of *Binaural* extends beyond its sales, for it was on the tour to support it that Pearl Jam launched their *Official Bootleg* series (see the Live Albums section). Every concert from the tour was recorded and released to retail, to prevent price-gouging by bootleggers. This fan-friendly effort generated a lot of goodwill for the band, and established a precedent for other acts to follow.

## 'Breakerfall' (Vedder)

The album blasts off with Pete Townsend-style power chords and a rockabilly bass line. But when the riff kicks in, it's strangely thin and brittle. Random bursts of electronic noise and deep distorted backing vocals are disorienting. It's as if the song has no centre to it. This song is an effective introduction to the album in one way at least: it prepares you for the unexpected. Vedder's double-tracked vocals are about the most assertive he will sound for the whole album. He sings of a girl who blames everyone but herself for her ennui: a short but effective character sketch.

## 'God's Dice' (Ament)

This is another full-tilt rocker without an easily identifiable riff or melody. The middle-eight breakdown doesn't clarify matters, as Vedder mumbles his way through it. And where a guitar solo should be, there are only howls of feedback. It's enjoyable noise, but it's still mostly noise.

## 'Evacuation' (Cameron, Vedder)

A more-clearly-defined central riff and a varying time signature distinguish this song from the preceding tracks. But strung together at the start of the album as they are, these three short rockers bleed together and wind up feeling like an overture to the album proper. Cameron makes his presence felt for the first time with his precisely off-kilter tub-thumping. For all this album's faults, the drum sound is excellent throughout.

## 'Light Years' (Gossard, McCready, Vedder)

This song should've been a killer. All the elements are present and accounted for, but none of them are pushed to where they need to be. The steady drum rhythm builds anticipation, and hesitant guitar notes gradually raise the energy level. But just when things seem primed to explode on the chorus, the murky mix and Vedder's mannered performance, rein it in. He sings in a fluttery almost-falsetto at times, and seems to be stumbling over his own breath to get the words out, as if he's on the verge of tears as he sings the chorus. But the chorus as written, cries out for the unabashed Vedder of 'Dissident' and 'Better Man'. When the guitar solo arrives, it sounds watery and weary instead of cathartic. Why the band decided to remix *Ten* and not *this*, is a mystery. 'Light Years' was *Binaural*'s second single, and it was not a notable hit. It sounds like it should be a live staple, but it has been performed less than 100 times.

All that said, the song's bones are so solid that it's still a good listen. Plus, Vedder's lyrics are some of his most evocative. He captures the sense of sad frustration that comes with losing someone unexpectedly. He can figure out games and riddles, but he can't explain how someone can die suddenly. As a comfort, he imagines that from up in heaven, the light of their soul reflects back on us.

## 'Nothing As It Seems' (Ament)

If you had asked a punter in 2000 what kind of single Pearl Jam should put out to follow the tragicomic 1960s cover that was their biggest ever hit, the answer would not have been 'A moody five-minute Pink Floyd pastiche'. If Pearl Jam wanted to deliberately sabotage their career, they couldn't have picked a better single. On the other hand, if they wanted to cement their standing as alt-rock's iconoclastic last-men-standing, they also couldn't have picked a better single.

Ament's lyrics are a series of sinister phrases without any clear throughline. They resemble the aleatory cut-up lyric-writing approach that Radiohead's Thom Yorke also used. Ament told MTV that the song is about reflecting on one's childhood and realising that not everything was as rosy as remembered. For once on this album, Vedder's mumbling vocal fits the song perfectly. He sounds almost befuddled, like the creeping sense of dread is overwhelming him. The music is incredibly effective at building that dread. Ament uses fretless bass once again, and gives the music a cavernous feel. The contrast between the distant bass rumble and the up-front acoustic guitar aids that sense of scale. But the real star of the show is Mike McCready on lead guitar. The moment at 1:50 when his guitar shifts from murky low notes to a soaring David Gilmour-esque tone, is magical. Then the breakdown after three minutes sees him bust out all the moves he honed on stage during 'Porch' and 'Crazy Mary'. Consider this song a taste of what non-concertgoers are missing.

### 'Thin Air' (Gossard)

The album has finally come alive. This is the third quality song in a row, even if it also seems a little underdeveloped. It's an unassuming folksy shuffle, like something from a mid-1970s Eric Clapton album. It's an ode to a girl, and the line 'I know she's reached my heart in thin air' is effectively enigmatic in a romantic way. The sharp little guitar lick a minute in, is the song's best moment, and it's a shame it's not repeated.

### 'Insignificance' (Vedder)

Ominous chords and rumbling drums introduce this mean-spirited song about small-town folk facing the apocalypse. Vedder told *George* magazine that it's about the inefficacy of protesting. Musically, it's an odd choice that the chords go up as the chorus goes 'Bombs dropping down', but it works. The lead-up to the chorus – a stabbing two-note riff accentuated by drums like gunshots – made the song come alive on stage. It's a pity the rest of the track lacks that dynamism, as Vedder's mumbling vocals again keep it grounded when it could soar. The frantic guitar riffing after the 3:45 mark is the closest this song comes to a climax.

### 'Of The Girl' (Gossard)

The album's hidden gem is this raga-like number about a man pining for the woman he left behind. If there's one song here that justifies Tchad Blake's involvement, it's this song. It's one where the binaural recording technique actually makes sense, as it does feel like you are sitting in on a jam session. Crackling blues licks in the background, create a firelight late-night feel.

### 'Grievance' (Vedder)

This song can't seem to decide what it wants to be from moment to moment. A moody opening gives way to punkish verses and a chorus that seems to disappear even as you're listening to it. This is the quintessential example of a filler track, in that the album would be stronger without it. That it was nominated for the Grammy for Best Hard Rock Performance, says more about the Grammy voters' tastes than it does about the quality of the song. The lyrics are about how modern technology that's supposed to make our lives easier, winds up enslaving us in other ways. Leave that sort of thing to Radiohead, Ed.

### 'Rival' (Gossard)

This is another song that's less than the sum of its parts, but this time the parts are a little more interesting. The sound of an angry dog (credited to

Dakota) leads into a two-note riff that can only be described as snarling. The multitracked vocals feel like they're trying to force a sense of drama that isn't there. On the other hand, the pounding piano – presumably played by Blake's frequent collaborator and Crowded House producer (and future member) Mitchell Froom – is effective at stringing out the tension. Lyrically it's a return to the theme of 'Jeremy'. The Columbine High School shooting of 1999 had brought gun violence back into the US political discourse, and it was dispiriting how little was done to prevent future shootings. This song considers the issue from a more ironic perspective than 'Jeramy' did, noting how the violence is often driven by ego.

### 'Sleight Of Hand' (Ament, Vedder)
With its fantastic, gated drum sound and 5/4 time signature, this is one of the album's best showcases for what Matt Cameron could bring to the band. While it's too obtuse to be called a great song, it's certainly an effective mood piece. The trilling guitar riff sounds like psychedelia by way of Tchaikovsky's 'Nutcracker Suite': like half-glimpsed fairies fluttering through the night. The big crunching chorus breaks the spell before the dreamlike instrumental break brings it back. The subject of the song seems to be a man who feels like he's lost himself in his social role: 'A time to dream to himself/He waves goodbye to himself'.

### 'Soon Forget' (Vedder)
Here we have the first appearance on a Pearl Jam album of the ukulele: an instrument Vedder would grow attached to (See the Solo Albums & Side Projects section). The song is a cute character sketch of a man whose materialistic priorities undermine his happiness. It's the kind of quirky social commentary that Ray Davies made a whole career out of.

### 'Parting Ways' (Vedder)
A tribal rhythm and guitars like sitars, harken back to *No Code*. The lyric's theme – two lovers on the brink of a breakup – makes it a suitable album closer. At minute two, strings add an extra layer of sad sweetness. While it's quite lovely, it would have more emotional punch if it closed off a more engaging and openhearted album.

This album's hidden track – known as 'Writer's Block' – is the sound of multiple typewriters being slammed. By the infinite monkeys perhaps?

# Riot Act (2002)

Personnel:
Jeff Ament: bass
Matt Cameron: drums, percussion, rhythm guitar
Stone Gossard, Mike McCready: guitar
Eddie Vedder: vocals, guitar
With:
Boom Gasper: Hammon organ, electric piano
Adam Kasper: piano
Producer: Adam Kasper
Recorded at Studio X, Seattle, Washington, February and May 2002
Release date: 12 November 2002
Chart places: US: 5, UK: 34
Running time: 54:15

The recording of the seventh album took place in the shadow of two tragedies – one deeply personal to the band and one on a scale previously unimaginable. The World Trade Center attack on 9 September 2001 spawned a cultural atmosphere of paranoia, jingoism and partisan hostility. A politically engaged band like Pearl Jam couldn't help but be affected by the general air of paranoia and rage. Closer to the band was the death of nine fans at the 30 June 2000 Roskilde Festival in Denmark. During Pearl Jam's set, a crowd crush occurred, some fans were accidentally dogpiled, and nine died from asphyxiation. The band were horrified, cancelling the final two dates of their European tour. Initially, some in the media tried to blame them for the tragedy; this was just a year after the Woodstock '99 festival broke out in violence that was partly attributable to Limp Bizkit goading the crowd. The Roskilde police cleared Pearl Jam of any wrongdoing. It took longer for them to reconcile with the event, and they seriously considered retiring. When they decided to press on with their 2001 North American tour, they left 'Alive' off the setlist until the final night in Seattle.

When the band reconvened after the *Binaural* tour, they once again brought in pieces they had created separately and worked them into complete songs. Despite the clouds hanging over them, the atmosphere in the sessions was quite positive. Cameron was now fully integrated into the band, Vedder had found his muse again, and McCready had undergone rehabilitation for prescription-drug addiction. They also worked with new producer Adam Kasper, who'd worked with Cameron's other bands. Unlike Tchad Blake, Kasper didn't impose his own sonic imprint on the band's sound. He created a relaxed atmosphere for them to lay down songs before they second-guessed themselves. Another addition was keyboardist Kenneth 'Boom' Gasper, who Vedder met in Hawaii. They gelled while jamming together, so Vedder invited him to play on the album. Gasper played on Pearl Jam's next three albums, and now serves as their live keyboardist. His solo on 'Crazy Mary' has become a concert highlight.

As for the album *Riot Act*, it's an improvement on *Binaural* in terms of warmth and accessibility. It has a less laboured-over feel, and its more-experimental tracks feel like part of the whole instead of weird tangents. However, there simply aren't that many memorable hooks and melodies. Also, while it isn't their longest album, it has the highest number of songs, at 15. That's at least three too many. In my opinion, it would be a stronger album without 'Cropduster', 'Ghost' and 'Green Disease'. I'm not a fan of 'Bu$hleaguer' either, but at least it's a historical curio.

The cover art is of two metal figurines wearing crowns: symbolism that seems to have no deeper meaning. It suggests the band were seeing off pretenders to their throne, or maybe that they felt they were pretenders themselves. The album title likewise lacks significance: it was decided on because they lacked a better option.

*Riot Act* was released alongside performance videos filmed at Seattle's Chop Suey club for the songs 'I Am Mine', 'Save You', 'Love Boat Captain', 'Thumbing My Way', and '1/2 Full'. The album reached the top 10 in various countries around the world. It was especially successful in Australia, perhaps because the album's best song 'Love Boat Captain' was released as a single there. But it only reached 5 in the US, and it was their second album in a row to not go platinum. It also reached a pitiful 34 in the UK: their lowest ever album chart peak in the English-speaking world. Again, we could blame the changing times, but I think even the band realised after this album that they needed a musical recalibration.

### 'Can't Keep' (Vedder)

This is Pearl Jam's most downbeat album opener so far. The martial drum rhythm grounds the song, while the psychedelic lead guitar swirls hint at a flight of fancy that never arrives. Vedder sings of self-discovery and his desire to not be held down. 'You can't keep me here' he says. So it's ironic that the song feels like it's circling around, when it should be taking off.

### 'Save You' (Ament, Cameron, Gossard, McCready, Vedder)

This mid-tempo rocker was an odd choice for a single, as the only thing that distinguishes it from the weaker tracks on *Binaural* is the profanity in the chorus. Thematically it's interesting, as Vedder declares he'll be there to help someone in need no matter what abuse they hurl at him. I imagine that's a sentiment he and the band hold tight, given everything they've gone through. So, it's a pity the song itself isn't more memorable. The riff feels curiously blunted, and Vedder doesn't unleash the fury the song demands. Predictably, it didn't go far as a single.

### 'Love Boat Captain' (Vedder, Boom Gasper)

This is possibly the best song the band recorded in the 2000s, and it's baffling that it was never released as a single in the United States. While it likely would not have done well on the charts in the Clear Channel playlist era, it would've received a little more attention. At the very least, it should've been included on Pearl Jam's *Greatest Hits* collection.

It's a tribute to the fans who died at Roskilde, and fittingly the band forgo their recent tendency to equivocate. They wear their hearts on their sleeves, and the song is all the better for it. The key line comes halfway through: 'Lost nine friends we'll never know/Two years ago today'. Vedder clearly felt a kind of survivor's guilt that these young people died trying to see him perform and that they were unknown to him until they died. He resolves this feeling by concluding that we are all ultimately strangers to each other: "Cause to the human race, I don't mean a thing'. The chorus is as terrifying as it is moving, with Vedder declaring that in a universe devoid of intrinsic meaning, the only thing that matters is that we love each other. Vedder acknowledges that his message has been said before, by quoting The Beatles' 'All You Need Is Love'. Sometimes it's simple sentiments like this that we need in times of turmoil.

Vedder told *The New Zealand Herald* that he intended this song to counteract the negativity the youth are constantly bombarded with. When he refers to 'the young' losing hope, it's a tacit acknowledgement that Pearl Jam are no longer the voice of youth. It's a subtle watershed moment for the band, as there's nothing more embarrassing than an artist who refuses to act their age because they still think they embody the zeitgeist.

The music was co-written by Boom Gasper during one of his original Hawaiian jam sessions with Vedder, and his organ-playing is undoubtedly the star of the show. But the entire band deliver a well-judged performance, pitched perfectly at that sweet spot where arena-rock moves elevate heartfelt emotions rather than smother them.

## 'Cropduster' (Cameron, Vedder)

Matt Cameron compositions often have an unusual rhythmic meter, and this song is a good example: the intro is two bars of 6/4 followed by one of 9/8. The verses are in 7/8 with occasional 2/4 bars along the way. The music spirals out from the intriguing opening riff, but it never settles into an identifiable melody or hook. The lead guitar fills after the first chorus, are the highlight. Lyrically, Vedder vents his frustration that the world hasn't turned out like he once imagined it would. The music does evoke a sense of despondency, though that's not a good thing in this case.

## 'Ghost' (Ament, Vedder)

This is another underwhelming rocker, based around a simple two-chord riff. Vedder sounds almost bored as he sings generic lyrics about urban disillusionment. Once again, the lead guitar is the highlight, *nay*, the song's saving grace.

## 'I Am Mine' (Vedder)

This song was a far more radio-friendly choice for a lead single than 'Nothing As It Seems', but it is odd in its own way. It opens with a tight little riff that leads straight into the melody. It has the rhythm of a sea shanty, but compared to 'Song X' it's easy to sing along to. The entry of the organ after the first chorus adds a real sense of drama: once again Gasper is the secret weapon. The climactic guitar solo is so sweet and well-constructed that you can't help but wish it went on longer.

This is another song of independence. But the difference between this and 'Given To Fly', is that this comes across as more combative, thanks to lyrics such as 'I know I was born and I know that I'll die' and 'I only own my mind'. Vedder initially sounds like he's gearing up for a fight, but in the second half he gets more contemplative. The song was written in the aftermath of the Roskilde tragedy, and it seems like Vedder needed to reassure himself that ultimately, he is answerable to himself. Other lines – like 'The north is to south what the clock is to time' – manage the R.E.M. trick of reading like gibberish but sounding profound in the moment.

This wasn't a huge hit single, but it got a fair amount of attention on the then-burgeoning musical blogosphere because its release was accompanied by Pearl Jam's first music video since 'Do the Evolution': a well-filmed straightforward performance clip.

### 'Thumbing My Way' (Vedder)
This was Pearl Jam's best acoustic track in years, and that can be attributed to the speed at which it was written and recorded. The raw-sounding acoustic guitar gives it the spontaneous feel of a campfire sing-along. Vedder's laid-back singing style suits the song perfectly, and as the rest of the band join in, the communal feel intensifies. The lyrics use hitchhiking as a metaphor for navigating past your regrets. There are trace elements of Robert Johnson's haunted country blues, especially in the line 'I can't be free with what's locked inside of me'. I doubt the band would appreciate the comparison, but this sounds quite like Guns N' Roses' 'Patience'.

### 'You Are' (Cameron, Vedder)
This is the album's most experimental track. The use of a triggered noise gate on the guitar gives this song a jittery stop-start pulse. It manages to sound simultaneously dream-like and robotic. Vedder sounds like he's scrambling to claw his way out of the machine. His lyrics go beyond a simple declaration of love; it's more like he's in awe of the power they hold over him.

### 'Get Right' (Cameron)
This is the album's best rocker, although it still isn't that great. The buzzing riff and Vedder's deadpan tone seem to flow from the robotic feel of 'You Are'. There is virtue in simplicity, but that doesn't include Cameron's lyric, which is mostly a string of Dylan-esque non-sequiturs.

### 'Green Disease' (Vedder)
This is another song based around a simple chugging riff, but this time there's little sense of space or dynamics. Aside from the trilling Peter Buck-like guitar

figure that kicks it off, it's unmemorable. The chorus tries to rise up out of the murk, but not hard enough to elevate the song. The lyrics are an opaque anti greed screed, but they include the album's best couplet: 'Tell the captain 'The boat's not safe and we're drowning'/Turns out he's the one making waves'.

## 'Help Help' (Ament)

With Vedder's multitracked high-pitched vocals, this song's feel is similar to Soundgarden's 'Half', so you might think Cameron wrote it. However, it's another of Ament's obtuse little ditties. There are barely any lyrics here. 'Tell me lies, tell me why', Vedder repeats before the chorus of 'Help me'. It doesn't sound desperate enough.

## 'Bu$hleaguer' (Gossard, Vedder)

Like many left-leaning people in the early 2000s, Pearl Jam were frustrated by the highly-contested 2000 presidential election, and disgusted by President George W. Bush's right-wing rhetoric. There's a long history of musicians writing songs against the President, and like most musicians who tried that, Pearl Jam fell flat on their faces.

The plodding rhythm and wailing guitar, sound petulant rather than incensed. The song twists its way through several sections without ever settling on a definable melody. If you want your audience to cheer along as you speak truth-to-power, you need to give them something catchy to chant. This song comes across as rambling and unfocused, with Vedder muttering strained baseball metaphors. The line 'Born on third, thinks he hit a triple' is an incisive summation of Bush's career, but after that, the song descends into ineffective abstraction. Compare this song to the music being made around the same time by bands like Anti-Flag and System Of A Down, who laid out the facts to furiously catchy riff rock. Compared to them, 'Bu$hleager' sounds like the worst kind of self-indulgent prog rock. You can see that even in the title's dollar sign – Do you get it? It's because Bush is rich! Is your mind blown yet?

When the US invaded Iraq during the North American leg of the *Riot Act* tour, this song became a protest against Bush's war on terror. Vedder performed the song while wearing a rubber mask of Bush's face, which he would toss around and abuse. This led to a backlash from right-wing media pundits, and fans who must not have known much about the band. This was at the same time the country music establishment blacklisted The Dixie Chicks for daring to disparage Bush. To musicians like them who dared express a political opinion, people said 'Shut up and sing'. In Pearl Jam's case, they should've sung us a powerful protest song, instead of this.

## '1/2 Full' (Ament)

This is the album's big guitar showcase. Like 'Red Mosquito', it opens with a guitar solo in full flight. The swing rhythm, Vedder's drawn out notes and the excessive wah-wah guitar, all contribute to a beleaguered hungover feeling. It's artless but fun. The lines that grab attention, are 'Don't see some men as half empty/See them half full of shit'. But more interesting is the line repurposed from 'Porch': 'There ain't going to be no middle anymore'. This time, the line refers to the vanishing American middle class.

## 'Arc' (Vedder)
This short wordless vocal piece shows the belated influence of Nusrat Fateh Ali Khan, who Vedder sang with on the *Dead Man Walking* soundtrack. It might also have been inspired by the wordless songs on David Crosby's *If I Could Only Remember My Name*. 'Arc' is a wondrous piece of music, with multiple layers of Vedder's voice merging together in a spiritual chant. It's another worthy tribute to the Roskilde victims, expressing without words the sorrow felt by everyone involved.

## 'All Or None' (Gossard, Vedder)
This is the least-good Pearl Jam closing track thus far, although it's a solid song in and of itself. It has a funeral pace and is mournful, contrasting with the lyric's message of endurance against the odds. McCready contributes two short but powerful guitar solos. The first has a tone reminiscent of Jimmy Page's circa Led Zeppelin's *Physical Graffiti,* while the closing solo is closer to McCready's work on 'Nothing As It Seems' and is a reminder of what this band is capable of when they free themselves from self-imposed restraints.

There's no hidden track this time, more's the pity.

# Lost Dogs (2003)

Personnel:
Dave Abbruzzese: drums
Jeff Ament: bass, guitar, vocals
Matt Cameron: drums, percussion, guitar
Stone Gossard: guitar, vocals, bass, percussion
Jack Irons: drums, guitar, vocals, percussion
Dave Krusen: drums
Mike McCready: guitar, piano
Eddie Vedder: lead vocals, guitar, harmonica
With:
Brendan O'Brien: guitar
Tchad Blake: Wurlitzer
Mitchell Froom: keyboards
Produced between 1991 and 2003
Release date: 11 November 2003
Chart places: US: 15, UK: 91
Running time: 111:55

To wind up their contract with Epic Records, Pearl Jam released two compilation albums. The first of these was mana to hardcore fans, as it collected most of Pearl Jam's original B-sides, some unreleased outtakes, compilation tracks, and a few of their Christmas-club singles, including their biggest hit. Often, a retrospective compilation is a sign that a band has given up on advancing their career. But when that band has enough leftover material to fill not one but *two* CDs, it seems more like a victory lap.

That said, *Lost Dogs* isn't wholly satisfying. For one thing, they didn't include *every* original B-side or Christmas single (see the The Ten Club holiday singles and Extras sections). Furthermore, many tracks were edited or partly re-recorded, meaning obsessives still had to track down the physical singles to get the original versions. But the music that *is* included is mostly great, although there are no revelations akin to 'Blind Willie McTell' on Bob Dylan's *Bootleg Series*. The unreleased tracks shed no new light on the band's thought processes, nor provide an alternate history of their musical development; they are mostly just pleasant reminders of how good Pearl Jam are even on their off days. A third of the outtakes are from 2000-2002, and these are the most interesting. None of them are exponentially better than what was included on *Binaural* and *Riot Act*, but as a whole, they suggest slightly more *rocking* versions of those albums.

This album is not sequenced chronologically, which is annoying if you're a Pearl Jam historian, but it makes for a better listen. The band wanted this to sound like a proper Pearl Jam album and not like a begrudging contractual-obligation floor-mopping exercise. That said, once you're past 'Last Kiss', you're into the dregs. The booklet includes comments from the band members on all the songs: some insightful, some perfunctory.

This collection debuted at 15 on the US album chart, and eventually went gold: a fine showing for what is essentially a collector's item.

### 'All Night' (Ament, Gossard, Irons, McCready, Vedder)

This is a previously unreleased outtake from *No Code*. The lyrics are fragmentary but seem to be about Vedder's sense that people don't care enough about politics. It's a rocker that manages to be simultaneously upbeat and downbeat. It wastes no time getting to a wild wah-wah guitar solo. But the lethargic vocals make for an unsettling contrast. It's as if the band are forcing themselves to stay awake. As it fades out, the massed backing vocals overwhelm the music, and it feels as if we're slipping into a dream. That makes for a good introduction to this *parallel universe* version of the band.

### 'Sad' (Vedder)

Another previously unreleased song, this time from the *Binaural* sessions. It gets off to a promising start with an Arabic-sounding guitar riff. But that's the song's most memorable aspect because the melody goes nowhere. Even the guitar solo seems perfunctory. The lyrics are more interesting, being a detailed description of a man grieving for the loss of a loved one. There are theories as to the song's deeper meaning, but I want an explanation for why it closes with a snatch of what sounds like klezmer music!

### 'Down' (Gossard, McCready, Vedder)

This was a B-side for 'I Am Mine'. The bouncy melody coupled with the Byrds-like guitar-playing make it sound like something Crowded House could've recorded. That band were an unsung influence on the 1990s alt-rock scene. Vedder decided against this song for inclusion on *Riot Act* because it didn't fit the album. But that's precisely why it would've improved it! Vedder still liked the song, and his lyric evokes the urge to overcome depression. He cites the title of historian Howard Zinn's autobiography – 'You can't be neutral on a moving train': In other words, eventually you have to face up to what's holding you down.

### 'Hitchhiker' (Vedder)

Another unreleased outtake from *Binaural*. This could've replaced 'Evacuation' or 'God's Dice', as it's far more immediate sounding. But maybe I'm grading on a curve because the opening is so great: 'You fool', Vedder cries as the music goes straight into overdrive. There is a mid-song breakdown that goes nowhere, but Cameron gets to show off his prowess in the buildup to the third verse. The combination of his wild drumming and the guitarists' swirling feedback is reminiscent of Pink Floyd circa *Ummagumma*, and sure enough, the band played 'Interstellar Overdrive' frequently during the Binaural tour. Lyrically, 'Hitchhiker' seems to be about the dangers of asking someone else to shoulder your emotional burdens.

## 'Don't Gimme No Lip' (Gossard)

This unreleased *No Code* outtake has a great title, a pleasingly brain-dead riff, and not much else. It's notable for being the only Pearl Jam song besides 'Mankind' with a lead vocal by Gossard. The title is a common expression, but it may nevertheless have been inspired by 'Don't Gimme No Lip Child': the 1964 Dave Berry B-side that was covered by the Sex Pistols. It has a similar garage band belligerence.

## 'Alone' (Abbruzzese, Ament, Gossard, McCready, Vedder)

This hesitant jam was a B-side for 'Go', although the music was written during the *Ten* sessions. Abbruzzese gets a credit because the band shared the music publishing when this song was released. For this compilation, Vedder re-recorded his vocal with amended lyrics, but this is still lyrically heavy-handed in a way that Pearl Jam had outgrown by the time of *Vs.*. Vedder describes a man's suicidal thoughts following a breakup: with all the subtlety of an after-school special, using hot coals and seagulls as metaphors. That said, the lines 'Does he fly away or just talk about it?' and 'I can help myself/Don't talk to me' acknowledge that one thing that can help people with suicidal thoughts, is to communicate their problems to someone sympathetic.

## 'In The Moonlight' (Cameron)

Another unreleased *Binaural* outtake, and another song that should've been included on that album. This demented swamp blues could only be the work of Matt Cameron. It seems to change the time signature every other bar, but never loses its base funkiness. His lyrics are quite evocative: an impressionistic mix of star and sea metaphors.

## 'Education' (Vedder)

Yet another unreleased *Binaural* outtake, and guess what?: it could've improved that album had it been included. It's a 1960s-sounding song. Lyrically, it questions whether the things we're taught at school actually help us in the real world: a very Dylan-ish concern. Musically it's reminiscent of Cream: from the tribal drum rhythm à la 'N.S.U.' to the sound of the guitar solo, which resembles Eric Clapton's fabled 'woman tone'.

## 'Black, Red, Yellow' (Vedder)

This song was originally released as a B-side of 'Hail, Hail', but this edit is half a minute longer. Despite its garage rock sound and stop/start structure, it would've seemed like light relief had it been included on *No Code*. It's a tribute to the flamboyant basketball player Dennis Rodman, who was a friend of the band. The title refers to the colours of his Chicago Bulls jersey. In lieu of a solo, there's a breakdown over which you can hear an answering machine message from Rodman, sounding like he's trying to arrange a meetup.

## 'You' (Vedder)

This is a reworked version of the B-side to 'Wishlist', and it would not have fitted on *Yield*. It's simple, but not in a good way like the A-side. It's an almost embarrassingly unabashed love song. The chorus consists of Vedder crying 'It's you' over and over. There's lots of energy, but no depth. Intermittently, there's the sound of what seems to be a fiddle, but it's not credited anywhere. It gives the song a slight country barn dance feel, and makes one wish they used that instrument more often.

## 'Leaving Here' (Holland, Dozier, Holland)

There are two stories to tell about this song. I'll tell the pleasant story first. 'Leaving Here' is an obscure Motown song from 1963 by the legendary Holland/Dozier/Holland songwriting team. It was not a notable hit when first recorded by lyricist Eddie Holland. But The Who recorded a version of it in 1965, and it has since become a garage-rock staple. Like most of the great Motown songs, it develops a simple idea to its fullest extent. Lyrically it's about how the men of the town better stop mistreating their women, or else they'll all be leaving. Musically it uses a call-and-response structure that gives the singer a chance to really ham it up. Pearl Jam make the most of it. The band pull the classic rock-and-roll trick of giving the guitarists two bars each in turn to solo. Vedder sings with raspy-voiced conviction, but the chirpy backing vocals keep this firmly in retro-rock territory.

Now for the sad story. This cover was originally released on a 1996 compilation album called *Home Alive: The Art of Self Defense*. This was released was to promote the organisation Home Alive – a Seattle non-profit founded to combat sexual assault, domestic violence, and provide self-defence training to people in need. Depending on your sense of irony, this choice of cover is either dead-on or tastelessly on the nose.

Home Alive was founded because of the 1993 rape and murder of Mia Zapata: the singer for Seattle punk band The Gits. Members of the Seattle music community – including Pearl Jam – contributed money to hire a private investigator to catch the killer. The funds eventually dried up, but the killer was caught and convicted in 2003 thanks to DNA evidence.

It's awful that the *Home Alive* compilation had to exist in the first place, but it remains an interesting historical artefact. Aside from Pearl Jam, it includes Seattle bigwigs Nirvana and Soundgarden, 1990s cult acts such as The Posies and The Presidents Of The United States Of America, riot grrrl bands like 7 Year Bitch, and rock legends Anne and Nancy Wilson and Joan Jett. This compilation also serves as an historical record of the alt-rock scene's unabashed feminism. Remember that not long after this, all these artists would lose their radio space to pop-punk bands complaining about their demanding girlfriends, emo bands complaining that they can't get a girlfriend, and nu metal bands complaining about the mere existence of women.

## 'Gremmie Out Of Control' (Haskell)

This is another cover version recorded for a charity album. It's a song by 1960s novelty act The Silly Surfers, and was included on *Music For Our Mother Ocean* – released in 1996 to support the Surfrider Foundation: a non-profit launched by Californian surfers to preserve beaches.

Given Vedder's love of surfing, it's odd that Pearl Jam have never written their own surf song in the old-school style of Dick Dale. But this cover is a convincing pastiche, with twangy guitars and excessive cymbal smashing. It's also the funniest song that Pearl Jam have ever recorded. The term 'gremmie' refers to an inexperienced surfer, and the lyrics detail how he is a danger to himself and others. Gossard provides the voice of the gremmie, yelling 'Cowabunga' in the background, while Vedder's deadpan vocal sounds close to 'Weird Al' Yankovic at times!

## 'Whale Song' (Irons)

This Irons original was released on the third *Music For Our Mother Ocean* compilation in 1999. By this time, the music more associated with surf culture was the laid-back folk pop of Ben Harper and Jack Johnson (both of whom would play live with Pearl Jam). There was a lot more emphasis on spiritualism in surf culture, hence this song: a musical expression of awe and wonder at the existence of the earth's largest mammals. Irons speak-sings some whale facts, such as that their heart is as big as a car and that 'They won't fight back' against the hunters and polluters. The band use bass swells and feedback to simulate the sound of whales talking under the ocean. There's a watery guitar solo that evokes oceanic bliss, followed by a piercing one that sounds a note of alarm. While it isn't a masterpiece or anything, this is one of the songs for which we should be grateful the *Lost Dogs* compilation rescued from obscurity.

## 'Undone' (Vedder)

This was the second B-side for 'I Am Mine'. It's a solid song with a bright bouncy riff. The false ending and climactic burst are excellent. The solo was done with an E-bow and features a Fripp-like sustain. Lyrically it's a straightforward expression of hope that the upcoming 2004 US presidential election would see the pendulum swing back towards Pearl Jam's side of the political spectrum.

## 'Hold On' (Gossard, Vedder)

This is an outtake from *Ten* (rather than *Vs.* as listed in the booklet). Vedder drones over generic riffage, blaming himself for a failed relationship (again). Any song from the *Ten* sessions will sound good by virtue of being from the *Ten* sessions, but this is musically lethargic and lyrically self-absorbed. It's the kind of thing that lesser Pearl Jam imitators such as Creed and Nickelback made their careers out of.

## 'YellowLedbetter' (Ament, McCready, Vedder)

One measure of a great musical artist is that they have an album track or B-side that's more intense and more ambitious than their big hits, and nevertheless becomes a fan favourite and a live showstopper. Springsteen has 'Jungleland', U2 have 'Bad', and Pearl Jam have 'Yellow Ledbetter'.

This was a B-side for 'Jeremy', and it was an instant hit with fans. It peaked at 21 on the Mainstream Rock Tracks chart based on airplay alone. In Australia, demand was such that the locally pressed single came with a sticker warning buyers to not waste money on the more-expensive import version. Its inclusion on this compilation was a no-brainer, but infuriatingly, the version included here cuts off the song's final note! So fans will still need to buy the single or the hits collection.

One thing that has kept this song locked in fans' hearts, is that – like Carly Simon's 'You're So Vain' – there's a mystery at its centre: namely, what the heck Vedder is even singing. His marble-mouthed singing is the source of many parodies and internet memes. This is one of the first songs Pearl Jam composed as a group, and Vedder made up the lyrics on the spot. There's never been an *official* lyric sheet published for this song, and he changes the words when singing it live. But it's not hard to figure out the broad strokes of the song's meaning: it's a lament for a friend or family member who was killed: presumably in war. One phrase that *is* understandable is 'The box or the bag': will he be coming home in a coffin or a body bag?

Like many a great rock song, it works on pure feel alone. Whatever Vedder is singing, you can tell he means it 100%. His wordless howls convey more than any poetic lyrics ever could. The band is equally powerful whilst also keeping things tasteful. McCready's opening riff is reminiscent of Jimi Hendrix's 'Little Wing'; a fragile fluttering thing that manages to retain its crystalline purity as Ament's swooping bass and Krushen's steady drums crash down upon it. At its heart, this is a blues, and that's no more evident than at the moment Vedder murmurs 'Make me cry' and McCready proceeds to do just that with one of the most emotive guitar solos ever preserved in digital bits.

'Yellow Ledbetter' is Pearl Jam's most frequent concert closer, and it never fails to leave the audience satisfied. McCready will often incorporate snatches of other songs – including 'Little Wing' – into the outro. But the best live recording in my opinion is the stripped-down version performed by just Vedder and McCready on the 1997 *Tibetan Freedom Concert* album, which was released to aid the cause of Tibetan independence.

Bizarrely, this was also the first Pearl Jam song licensed for use in a television show: in 2004 (!) for the *Friends* finale. It was also used with more distinction in the 2019 show *Stumptown*, where it accompanies a flashback that is basically the song's lyric in film form.

## 'Fatal' (Gossard)

Another *Binaural* outtake, this time one that arguably would not have made that album more accessible. This sounds like the first half of a potentially good song. Vedder under-sings it, and it just sort of winds down until it disappears. According to the liner notes, the original lyric was 'The answer's in Plato', but Vedder kept messing it up and instead we get 'The answers are fatal'.

## 'Other Side' (Ament)

The was a B-side for 'Save You'. It was written by Ament as a tribute to his parents, and is about one partner reflecting on the passing of the other. Given the subject matter, it seems churlish to say that this mid-tempo ballad is the closest Pearl Jam have come to sounding like the many drab MOR college rockers that followed in their wake. Its most distinguishing musical feature is the keyboard drone throughout the verses. Ament's lyric is occasionally interesting, but too often defaults to mediocre phrases like 'It's not the same without you' and 'You can't know what it's like'. I don't want to pick on a heartfelt song, but this is very much a B-side.

## 'Hard To Imagine' (Gossard, Vedder)

This was an outtake from the *Vs./Vitalogy* era, released on the soundtrack to the forgotten 1997 movie *Chicago Cab* (aka *Hellcab*). It's a gentle but insistent folk tune that shows the power of simplicity. It starts with a snake-charming guitar figure underpinned by the thump of a bass drum. Then the electric guitar and snare drum enter, and Vedder cuts loose with a soaring crescendo. It's lyrically sparse, but there are hints of perennial Vedder concerns such as the long-term impact of childhood trauma. The title refers to the scale of the unspecified ordeal the narrator endured. According to Gossard's liner notes, the band get many requests for this at concerts. This is one of the few *Lost Dogs* outtakes that could've improved *Vs.* or *Vitalogy*.

## 'Footsteps' (Gossard, Vedder)

The is the other B-side on the 'Jeremy' single, and it's one of the key *secret* songs in the band mythology. It was developed out of the same guitar figure that formed the basis of 'Times Of Trouble' from *Temple Of The Dog*, so it forms a bridge between that project and Pearl Jam. It was also one of the three songs on the demo tape that Gossard sent Vedder.

It is the third part of the *Momma-Son* trilogy, after 'Alive' and 'Once'. The first two detail the narrator's childhood trauma and his mental breakdown. On 'Footsteps', he is on death row reflecting on where it all went wrong. Vedder sings of isolation and self-harm, and when he cries 'It was you', he could be talking to his mother, the voices in his head or himself. The line 'Let me just continue to blame you' indicates he knows he's trying to deflect responsibility. You wouldn't know on the first listen that this is part of any multi-song narrative. But it's such a great example of dark Americana – drawing on classic prison songs and murder ballads – that the backstory is irrelevant. You could imagine Johnny Cash covering this on one of his *American...* albums.

There are two versions of 'Footsteps': the original single, and this version with harmonica, which I prefer because the harmonica adds a bluesy feeling. But without it, the song is starker and more chilling, so I can understand why some fans prefer that.

### 'Wash' (Ament, Gossard, Krusen, McCready, Vedder)

'Wash' was a B-side for 'Alive', and it was also included as a bonus track on some European editions of *Ten*. It's an ominous ballad with gorgeous bluesy guitar work and a commanding performance from Vedder. It opens evocatively with the line, 'Oh please let it rain today': an ironic wish for a Seattle resident. But this rain is symbolic: the narrator is tormented by his lustful thoughts, and he yearns for a spiritual cleansing. If this song wasn't so musically beautiful, I'd say it would be perfect on a soundtrack for a movie about a serial killer.

The version of 'Wash' on *Lost Dogs* is a different take. The main difference between the two is the production – the single version is sparse and sinister, while this version is dense and gothic. The *Lost Dogs* version wins for me, because the drum-free opening creates a spookier atmosphere. Either version could've been included on *Ten*, although mood-wise 'Wash' might be too similar to 'Garden'.

### 'Dead Man' (Vedder)

This was a B-side for 'Off He Goes', but was originally written for the movie *Dead Man Walking*. It was passed over in favour of a similarly-titled Bruce Springsteen song, which is fair enough. The lyrics are from the perspective of Sean Penn's character from that film: a death row inmate waiting to die. Vedder captures the feeling of overwhelming regret, but there's also a hint of bitterness ('They're all mocking me'). The song has an appropriately hushed and spooky feel. The moment about 30 seconds in when the ever-so-soft feedback rumble rises up, is magical.

### 'Strangest Tribe' (Gossard)

This was the band's 1999 Christmas fan club single. The festive element is the occasional sleigh bells. The lyrics are obtuse, but the title could be referring to the early Christians. The music has a comfy down-home feel, although Vedder is at his most tired-sounding. You could say it accurately evokes the feeling of being done with Christmas after all the gift-giving, eating and family business is done. The late-arriving electric piano is a nice touch, and it makes you wish they used that instrument more.

### 'Drifting' (Vedder)

Also from the 1999 Christmas single, this is a folksy sing-along with a timeless melody. The harmonica makes it sound like a folk standard that Bob Dylan could've covered in his Greenwich Village days. The lyrics cover similar territory to John Lennon's 'Imagine': the dream of divesting yourself of possessions and living free of material worries. While this song might've felt out of place on *Binaural*, it would've added some human warmth to that album's back half.

## 'Let Me Sleep' (McCready, Vedder)

This was their 1991 Christmas fan club single, and it's the best of that whole series. It's perfect in its simplicity, consisting of a sprightly guitar figure, hand percussion and Vedder's yearning vocal. It's also a minor miracle in being a Christmas song that avoids all mention of the usual yuletide signifiers such as Santa, snow, etc. Instead, it's a dark vignette about a homeless man (perhaps the same one from 'Even Flow') who remembers how magical Christmas felt when he was a child. It feels like something out of *A Christmas Carol*.

## 'Last Kiss' (Cochran)

Just as every great band has their 'Yellow Ledbetter', they also have their 'Last Kiss': a hit pop single that no hardcore fan will admit to liking. Resistance is futile in this case because this is a terrific song, and Pearl Jam's performance more than does it justice. There are many other Pearl Jam songs that deserved to be hit singles, but only a gatekeeping grumpy guts would begrudge this single its success.

The original was a teen-tragedy song from the golden age of such things. The original 1961 recording by Wayne Cochran even opens with squealing tires and a scream. The lyrics detail the fateful car accident that took the life of the narrator's girlfriend. Now he's determined to stay on the straight and narrow so he can see her again in heaven. Despite the ultimately wholesome message, Cochran's deadpan vocal and the minimal musical backing give the song a ghoulish feel. It's ridiculously camp, which makes Pearl Jam's version even more impressive. They play it completely straight, at a more natural tempo, with an in-the-pocket performance from Matt Cameron (in his studio debut with the band), and a fully committed performance from Vedder. The way his voice leaps out right from the first bar, no doubt helped this song grab radio listeners.

This was released as a non-album single, to support Kosovo refugees, and in reaching number 2 on the *Billboard* pop chart, it raised over $10,000,000. It's also available on the *No Boundaries: A Benefit For The Kosovar Refugees* compilation, along with its B-side 'Soldier Of Love' (see Extras).

## 'Sweet Lew' (Ament)

This *Binaural* outtake may be the most unpleasant song Pearl Jam have ever recorded. Even as a joke, it's still laboured and mean-spirited. It's a detailed and personal takedown of basketball legend Kareem Abdul-Jabbar, who apparently was indifferent when Ament introduced himself at a party. Ament – who sings lead here for the first and only time – should know better than most that celebrities don't owe you their time just because you're a fan.

This petulant song would be easier to take if it didn't sound like Primus on Quaaludes.

### 'Dirty Frank' (Abbruzzese, Ament, Gossard, McCready, Vedder)

This was a B-side of 'Even Flow', although this version is slightly longer and has much of the lyric removed. It was also another bonus track on some European editions of *Ten*. It *really* doesn't belong on that album, being inspired by their early tour with Red Hot Chili Peppers. On the surface, Pearl Jam share little in common with those L.A. party rockers. Jack Irons did play with both bands, but not on the albums that defined them. But these days it's forgotten that in the early-1990s the Chili Peppers were regarded as cutting-edge. They were part of the funk-metal wave that helped bridge the gap between hard rock and black music, and they sang with refreshing candour about subjects like heroin addiction. But, of course, they also wrote songs like 'Sir Psycho Sexy' and 'Suck My Kiss', and it's from that template that Pearl Jam made 'Dirty Frank'. Over a lunkheaded funk riff, Vedder raps about their bus driver being a cannibalistic serial killer. He throws in references to the theme from *Shaft*, and McCready is apparently eaten right there in the studio! Let's just say that, as a rapper, Vedder makes for a good surfer. But it's hard to dislike a song that's so unrepentantly goofy.

### 'Brother' (Instrumental version) (Gossard)

When *Lost Dogs* was being compiled, Gossard remained uninterested in finishing this *Ten* outtake, and Vedder was not happy with his lyric. So they stripped the vocals from the recording, and McCready recorded new lead guitar parts to fill the space. It was an awkward compromise and it sounds like it. Fortunately, Gossard and Vedder reconsidered, and a full vocal version was included on the *Ten* reissue.

### 'Bee Girl' (Ament, Vedder)

This was recorded on 18 October 1993 on the radio interview program *Rockline*. It's an anti-fame warning from Vedder, directed at child actress Heather DeLoach, who played the bee girl in the music video for the hit song 'No Rain' by Los Angeles alt-rock band Blind Melon. The video is a prime slice of 1990s hooray-for-the-outsiders schtick: DeLoach, dressed in a puffy bumblebee costume, is mocked and scorned as she tries to do her little tap dance, until she finds a hidden community of bee people dancing freely.

DeLoach made the most of her 15 minutes of fame – appearing as Bee Girl at the MTV Video Music Awards (the night Pearl Jam won for 'Jeremy'), and also in the video for 'Weird Al' Yankovic's Red Hot Chili Peppers spoof 'Bedrock Anthem'. DeLoach is a good example of a pre-internet viral video star. There's a sense that Vedder isn't calling her out specifically, but rather is using her as a stand-in for all children who are forced into the limelight. However, this song is off-puttingly didactic – especially when the first line is 'Bee girl, you're gonna die'. Is that a promise or a threat? Vedder's spoken-word section sounds like Neil Diamond at his most gauche. That said, the advice is sound.

## '4/20/02' (Vedder)

This *Riot Act* outtake is a hidden track that starts four minutes after 'Bee Girl' finishes. It's titled after the day Alice In Chains' Layne Stanley was found dead. The track was unlisted because the band didn't want to be seen as capitalising on his death in any way.

Alice In Chains were one of the biggest and most respected Seattle grunge bands, and Stanley – with his distinctive nasal voice – was an icon, though not always for the right reasons. His drug problems were well-documented, and after they caused his band to fall apart and he disappeared from view, there was a sense it was only a matter of time before he overdosed. And so it proved to be. This death hit the band hard – in part because McCready had worked with Stanley in the supergroup Mad Season (see Solo Albums & Side Projects), and also because of the tragic inevitability about it. You can't help someone who doesn't want to be helped, but that doesn't stop you from feeling you could've done more. Thus, this song is desperate sounding, clearly coming from a place of frustration. Vedder attacks his guitar Richie Havens style, and bookends a reflection on the loneliness of the drug user with two angry verses directed at all the post-grunge vocalists who ripped off Stanley's style. This is one of the few times Vedder explicitly called out his contemporaries in song.

# Rearviewmirror (Greatest Hits 1991-2003)

Pearl Jam wrapped up their contract with Epic Records by releasing this collection. It was a nice parting gift for the company; Pearl Jam's new music had become harder to market, so here was a chance to remind the public why they fell in love with the band, to begin with. Pearl Jam got in under the wire before these kinds of compilations went the way of the 8-track and the label sampler. By the mid-2000s, illegal file-sharing had caused the music industry to bottom out, so the record companies doubled down on guaranteed high-selling items like The Beatles *1* and Elvis Presley's *Elv1s: 30 No. 1 Hits*. There were already well-regarded compilations out there for Nirvana, Soundgarden and Alice In Chains, so it made sense for Pearl Jam to follow suit. However, they chose to do things a little differently. They released a two-CD set with one disc of rockers and one of ballads. In theory, this should highlight the band's multifaceted artistry, and counter them being pigeonholed as the angry young men of the *Time* magazine cover. In practice, it means the rockers disc is heavily weighted towards their early days, and includes a few songs that aren't really among their best ('Once', 'Go', 'Save You'), while the ballads disc doesn't have room for 'Love Boat Captain'. On the positive side, the selection highlights a few great album tracks that might've passed the casual fan by, such as 'Corduroy', 'Nothingman' and the title track.

Almost all hits collections include purchase incentives in the form of otherwise unavailable songs. *Rearviewmirror* doesn't include brand new gems comparable to, say, Tom Petty's 'Last Dance with Mary Jane' or Madonna's 'Vogue', but it does include the two songs from the *Singles* soundtrack, the non-album single 'Last Kiss' and the essential B-side 'Yellow Ledbetter' (which is the one song included out of chronological order: at the very end, which was a wise decision). The big selling point for hardcore fans was the Brendan O'Brien remixes of 'Once', 'Alive' and 'Black', which were a trial run for the full *Ten* remix. There are only two otherwise-unavailable songs which require elaboration.

### 'Even Flow' (Single version) (Gossard, Vedder)

This is not a remix, but a full re-recording that was used for the video and released as a single in Europe. It was recorded in 1992, so Abbruzzese is the drummer. He gives the song a slightly looser, funkier feel, but the drier production highlights the lyric's underlying anger. The most notable difference is Vedder's introductory yelp, for which, honestly, this version is worth owning.

### 'Man Of the Hour' (Vedder)

This subdued acoustic ballad was recorded in 2003 for *Big Fish*: Tim Burton's last good movie. Like the movie, it concerns a son saying goodbye to his father, and it perfectly captures the emotional push/pull of a contentious parent/child relationship. Whether it should be counted amongst Pearl Jam's best, depends on one's own relationship with one's father. It was released as a single on Pearl

Jam's website: their first self-released music. It did not chart but was nominated for a variety of film-music awards.

# **Pearl Jam** (2006)

Personnel:
Jeff Ament: bass
Matt Cameron: drums, percussion, backing vocals
Stone Gossard, Mike McCready: guitar
Eddie Vedder: lead vocals, guitar
With:
Boom Gasper: piano, Hammond organ, pump organ
Producer: Adam Kasper, Pearl Jam
Recorded at Studio X, Seattle, Washington, November 2004-February 2006
Release date: 2 May 2006
Chart places: US: 2, UK: 5
Running time: 49:44

*Rearviewmirror* and *Lost Dogs* reminded fans and critics of why Pearl Jam mattered. Moreover, a series of other releases between *Riot Act* and this album helped renew interest in all things grunge. In October 2002, the first *new* Nirvana song since 1993 – the outtake 'You Know You're Right' – was released, and was better than anyone could've hoped for. Ex-Nirvana member Dave Grohl played drums on the epochal *Songs for The Deaf* album by Queens Of The Stone Age, and he joined them on tour along with ex-Screaming Trees frontman Mark Lanegan. Meanwhile, Grohl's own band Foo Fighters kept up their string of gold-and-platinum-selling singles. Grohl wasn't the only grunge icon keeping the flame alive: not one but *two* alt-rock supergroups formed in the early 2000s. Chris Cornell of Soundgarden joined the instrumentalists from Rage Against the Machine to form Audioslave, and Scott Weiland of Stone Temple Pilots joined with a bunch of ex-Guns N' Roses musicians to form Velvet Revolver. While neither of these bands made music as good as the groups they came from, they each scored a few massive rock-radio hits before falling apart. So while grunge was gone, it was not forgotten, and when Pearl Jam returned with an album that eschewed experimental meandering for a straight-down-the-line hard-rock attack, they were welcomed with open arms.

The band seemed to have a fire under them, due to a variety of factors. George W. Bush's re-election and the ongoing war on terror inspired some of Vedder's most politically direct lyrics and his most powerful studio vocal performances in years. Pearl Jam participated in the 2004 Vote for Change tour to raise money for Democrat political action groups. Playing alongside luminaries like Bruce Springsteen, Jackson Browne, Neil Young, and newbies like Death Cab for Cutie, Bright Eyes and My Morning Jacket meant that Pearl Jam could no longer be considered outsiders. Now they were part of the chain linking classic roots rock with hip, modern indie rock.

Vedder's first child was born in 2004. While it isn't referenced in the lyrics, that sort of thing is bound to give someone a new perspective and encourage them to play to their strengths. The band also recaptured that sense of 'five against one' that made them great. On Matt Cameron's third album with the band, he became Pearl Jam's longest-serving drummer, and he sounded like he'd always been playing with them. They were now a well-drilled fully collaborative team. This album's songwriting was more democratic than any time since *Vs.*. The members arrived at the sessions with little but basic riffs. With Adam Kasper producing again, and Boom Gasper on keys, the band had clearly found their comfort zone.

If Pearl Jam's first three albums placed them squarely in the grunge category, and their next four saw them searching for an identity, this is the first that could really only be described as 'rock' – not grunge or alt-rock or any other category, but good old-fashioned rock and roll. The back-to-basics mentality is reflected in the eponymous album title. It's as if the band are reintroducing themselves. Some fans refer to this album as *Avocado*, after the baffling cover image. McCready told Michigan's *Grand Rapids Press* that the art was a random choice. Far more interesting are the booklet photos of the band members' faces, distorted and decaying, though these would also not have made a good cover. They might've made people think Pearl Jam had switched to black metal!

This album was issued in a one-off deal with J Records: a subsidiary of Sony Music at the time. It gave the band their best global chart placings since *Binaural*. In the US it was held off the top spot by the return of fellow-1990s alt-rock legends Tool. While *Pearl Jam* didn't sell in 1990s quantities, it let everyone know that the band weren't about to burn out *or* fade away.

## 'Life Wasted' (Gossard, Vedder)

This is Pearl Jam's most forceful album opener yet. There's no fade-in or warm-up: just a curt three-note riff before the pile-driving rhythm kicks in. The lyric reflects the don't-bore-us-get-to-the-chorus attitude: 'I've tasted a life wasted, and I ain't ever going back again'. With its irregular rhythm and stop/start structure, this *should* be a mess, but Vedder's performance holds it together. After half a decade of sounding in the studio like he was perturbed by what he was singing, he sounds fully-invested again

Part of that might be the song's inspiration: the 2004 death of Ramones guitarist Johnny Ramone, at age 55 from prostate cancer. Despite being an avowed republican, Johnny was close friends with many prominent left-leaning alt-rock figures, including Eddie Vedder. It was the drive back from Johnny's funeral that inspired Vedder's lyric. Despite his use of the second person, the lyric isn't directed at Johnny Ramone. When Vedder sings 'You're always saying you're too weak to be strong/You're harder on yourself than just about anyone', he's calling out us listeners for our complacency – stop making excuses; don't waste your life.

This was released as the album's second single. It didn't do especially well on the charts, but the video featuring life-size busts of the band members, being warped and manipulated, is cool in a disturbing way.

### 'World Wide Suicide' (Vedder)

This was Pearl Jam's most instantly appealing and crowd-pleasing lead single since 'Given To Fly' – a conscious return to the kind of sound that made people fall in love with them to begin with; not that it's a throwback or a cynical attempt to ape past glories: in 2006, *that* was U2's stock-in-trade. No, this is a rage-filled punk rocker; timeless in its simplicity, but extremely relevant to its time.

In 2006 – with ongoing wars, terrorist bombings, protests and social issues – it did seem as if the world was sliding into chaos. So this song title and chorus were relatable no matter what side of the political spectrum you were on. The verses are specifically about losing a soldier friend, and the hypocrisy of the government praising the military while treating them as disposable. Vedder was inspired by the case of Pat Tillman – an ex-pro-footballer who joined the army following the 9/11 attacks, and whose death by friendly fire the government tried to hush up.

The music sounds righteously angry, thanks to Cameron's heart-pounding drums and Vedder, Gossard and McCready's ferocious three-guitar attack. The light middle eight and the despairing-yet-hopeful vocal, leavens the fury a little. Vedder harmonises with himself, and the moment in the second verse where one of his vocals continues the song while the other wails in the background, is pure magic; so is the moment after the middle eight when the guitar skitters along like a buzzing engine for a few bars.

This single was only released digitally, so there only seems to be records for the US chart placing. In its first week, it was played almost 2000 times on alternative/modern-rock radio, and so it became Pearl Jam's best-performing (non-cover) single since 'Given To Fly'. It spent three weeks at number 1 on the US rock radio chart, and was apparently the first digitally-delivered chart-topper in Canada. It seems the band remembered the first rule of showbiz: give the people what they want.

### 'Comatose' (Gossard, McCready, Vedder)

This is the third hard rocker in a row, and while it's a step down from the previous two, its chorus is just as powerful. With a more murky mix, this could've suited *Vitalogy*. The harmonised guitar melody leading into the second verse is straight out of the Thin Lizzy playbook, while the short wiggly guitar solo is pure Seattle grunge. Vedder's lyric refers to being isolated and/or insensible, but this is framed almost as a good thing, as it removes his fear of failure. Whatever it means, it rocks.

### 'Severed Hand' (Vedder)

There's a brief respite as this song fades in with skittering drums that sound like a huge machine warming up. Then the song explodes into a funk-inflected riff that's the tightest the band has sounded in years. The middle-eight melody is the song's strongest part. It's superficially similar to the chorus of

'Insignificance', but here it sounds like calm amidst the storm. The guitar solo is a bit haphazard and it's mixed strangely low.

Vedder's vocal tracks pitched high and low give the song a slightly spooky feel, which fits the lyric: a dialogue between himself and some mysterious figure that's tempting him; with drugs perhaps: there is strange hallucinogenic imagery, including the title's severed hand. Also, this is the second song in a row where the world 'falling', features prominently. This combination of words and music gives the impression that Vedder feels a little out of control.

### 'Marker In The Sand' (McCready, Vedder)

You could be forgiven for confusing this song and the previous one. They're both based around furious choppy riffs contrasted with a gentler section: in this case, a chorus with a vague country feel. The lyric is about how the original messages of religions have been lost over the years, and now you have groups trying to kill each other, each claiming to be acting in God's name.

### 'Parachutes' (Gossard, Vedder)

The pace *finally* eases up! This slowed-down hoedown is reminiscent of Neil Young circa *Harvest*. Lyrically, it's hard to pin down. It's definitely a love song, but it's difficult to determine whether it's about missing someone, not needing someone, being grateful for their support (the parachute metaphor), or all three. Vedder's voice almost cracks as he reaches for the high notes, and that moment of vulnerability sells it better than the words do.

### 'Unemployable' (Cameron, McCready, Vedder)

This mid-tempo rocker has big Springsteen vibes: it covers similar thematic territory to his songs like 'Downbound Train' and 'My Hometown'. It's about a man who loses his job and feels cheated that he sacrificed so much for other people to get rich. This was written two years before the global financial crisis caused many people to ponder the exact same thing. Not since *Vs.* had Vedder written a character sketch as precise and vivid. The chorus is thin and too reliant on half-hearted 'oh-oh-oh''s, but the backing vocals manage to sell it. As with most of this album, the performance has a warmth that's hard to quantify.

### 'Big Wave' (Ament, Vedder)

Here is one last hard rocker before the album winds down. This song couldn't be simpler: it's a tribute to surfing. It manages to sound like surf music without having any of that music's identifiable elements, such as reverb-drenched drums and twangy guitar. The solo is particularly interesting – a wall of guitar noise through which a thin guitar melody flows: like the audio equivalent of surfing through a tubular wave. Then the rhythm switches up and the song fades out on a fractious jam that I would've been happy to hear continue for another five minutes.

## 'Gone' (Vedder)

This song should've followed 'Unemployable', as it feels like a continuation of it – a man disillusioned with the American dream, takes to the road to find something better. Vedder doesn't say exactly what he's looking for, only that he needs to escape the emptiness he feels. This song is cut from the same cloth as Simon & Garfunkel's 'America', Jackson Browne's 'Running on Empty' and Bob Seger's 'Against The Wind': songs where the open road embodies the freedom and potential we once had. In the outro, Vedder puts his own twist on a line from The Who's 'Let's See Action': 'If nothing is everything, I will have it all'. It's better to have all of nothing than a tiny piece of something that doesn't matter to you.

This track has fantastic dynamics. It builds from a taut acoustic guitar figure so pregnant with tension, to a roaring road anthem with thunderous tom-toms and crashing cymbal waves that sweep you up in the man's desire to escape. With a slightly stronger chorus (something more memorable than just the word 'gone' repeated), this could've been a proper epic. This was the album's third single: released via download.

## 'Wasted Reprise' (Gossard, Vedder)

Vedder sings the chorus of the opening track, accompanied only by fairground organ. It doesn't add much to the album, but it demonstrates what a strong hook that chorus is.

## 'Army Reserve' (Ament, Vedder, Damien Echols)

Time for another sad story, unfortunately. In 1993 in West Memphis, Arkansas, three eight-year-old boys were found murdered. Three teenage boys who had a reputation for nonconformity were accused of killing the boys as part of a satanic ritual. Certain of the teenagers' guilt, the police used coercive tactics to ensure they were convicted. The West Memphis Three were sentenced to – respectively – 40 years, life in prison, and death.

This miscarriage of justice became a cause célèbre for the alt-rock/metal world. It was felt that the teenagers were targeted because of their tastes in music and pop culture: a case of satanic panic. A series of documentaries called *Paradise Lost* drew attention to the case, and some compilations were released to raise money for the teenagers' legal defence. The first – *Free the West Memphis 3* – includes a cover of the song 'Poor Girl' by Los Angeles punk band X, performed by Vedder with Supersuckers.

I'm covering this because one of the West Memphis Three – Damien Echols – contributed lyrics to this song. Echols told the WM3.org website that he hoped the collaboration would bring more attention to the case. Eventually, in 2011, the three men were released from prison, after a plea deal which let their convictions stand without them admitting guilt. This was a rare case of celebrity activism having a tangible effect on the real world.

What's interesting is that this song has nothing to do with the West Memphis murders or legal malpractice or anything like that. It's about a woman whose husband is in the army, and she knows eventually she'll hear bad news, and she feels as if her child is already judging her. It's a different kind of anti war song to 'World Wide Suicide': its power comes from its finely-observed details about the psychological toll of war.

This song is also a quiet wonder musically. The album's best moment is the ringing opening riff: a deft alchemical mix of fluttery guitars that generate a feeling of longing and worry. The rest of the song doesn't quite live up to that introduction, but it's still strong. Vedder roars the chorus, and once again the backing vocals add a great deal of warmth.

## 'Come Back' (McCready, Vedder)

One of the things punk's furious onslaught did, was squeeze much of the blues influence out of rock music. This wasn't necessarily a bad thing, as by the end of the 1970s, what had once been fresh had become stale cliché. But one thing that was regrettably swept aside was a certain kind of sensitive, stately blue-eyed-soul ballad. Think The Rolling Stones' 'I Got The Blues', Faces' 'Debris' and most of Van Morrison's early repertoire. In the 1980s, hair-metal power ballads copped the blues moves but had none of the soul, and they were in turn displaced by doomy self-flagellating grunge ballads à la Pearl Jam's 'Black'. In the irony-drenched 1990s, rock stars were too self-conscious to go full crooner.

This song is arguably the closest Pearl Jam have come to sounding like those classic ballads, and it's just wonderful. It's a tale of romantic longing, as classic and timeless as the 'Stand By Me' chord changes. Vedder sounds the best he has on record since *Yield*. In any of his contemporaries' hands, this would've sounded mawkish. In fact, if Pearl Jam had attempted this on their second or third album, they would've sounded like pandering phonies. But now, their experience and discipline helped keep the song grounded in a place of humility. The only disappointment is the guitar solo, which is thin and waffling and only comes alive as Vedder returns for the final refrain. The wordless wooing in the climax, feels like a throwback to 'Black' in the best way.

## 'Inside Job' (McCready, Vedder)

Ominous distant wailing sets an intriguing tone for another strong album closer. The plaintive guitar notes over the opening acoustic strumming sound similar to Steve Hackett's work on Genesis' early-1970s albums. Meanwhile, Gasper's piano is reminiscent of Van Morrison's music – not playing a melody or a solo, but dropping-in random licks during quiet moments, for maximum drama. This is another example of how Pearl Jam have synthesised influences from all corners of the rock world. It's a surprisingly complicated song that uses over ten chords! They introduce some chords in the climax for maximum drama, and then there's a lovely little guitar melody on the outro.

This song is notable as being the first time McCready contributed lyrics to a Pearl Jam song. According to his *Grand Rapids Press* interview, he wrote the lyric to ensure the song got on the album, as Vedder didn't have anything for it. But the message of self-belief and standing firm in the face of adversity, is very much in keeping with Vedder's themes.

The hidden track this time is a very brief guitar piece that sounds like stars twinkling. It's a haunting ending to a powerful album.

# Backspacer (2009)

Personnel:
Jeff Ament: bass
Matt Cameron: drums, percussion
Stone Gossard, Mike McCready: guitar
Eddie Vedder: vocals, guitar
With:
Brendan O'Brien: piano, backing vocals
Bruce Andrus, Richard Deane, Susan Welty: horn
Justin Bruns, Christopher Pulgra: violin
Cathy Lynn: viola
Danny Laufer: cello
Producer: Brendan O'Brien
Recorded at Henson Studios, Los Angeles, California; Southern Tracks Studio,
Atlanta, Georgia, February-April 2009
Release date: 20 September 2009
Chart places: US: 1, UK: 9
Running time: 36:38

In 2007, Vedder released his first solo album: the soundtrack to Sean Penn's film *Into the Wild* (see Solo Albums & Side Projects). Critics of the band had long expected Vedder to break away and go solo, but this album was not a typical solo project; it was more of a meditative mood piece than a statement of artistic independence. No one doubted that Pearl Jam were still his primary vehicle.

The band began work on *Backspacer* after their 2006 tour concluded. Now that they were all family men with ongoing side projects, they reverted to recording demos separately and collaborated via email. They brought Brendan O'Brien back as producer. While he'd mixed *Riot Act* and parts of *Binaural*, this was his first time producing the band since *Yield*. In between then and *Backspacer*, O'Brien had produced four albums for Bruce Springsteen: one of which was his artistic and commercial post-9/11 triumph *The Rising*. Learning that even The Boss took suggestions from O'Brien, convinced the band to bring him back. They also spent some time recording outside Seattle for the first time since *No Code*, and this may have helped them get outside their own heads and ease up on the angst.

If the self-titled album was Pearl Jam proving they still had it, *Backspacer* is the sound of them settling comfortably into middle age. This isn't a criticism; every rock band has to eventually grow up. If they don't, the results aren't pretty (for example, Motley Crüe: in their 60s, still playing songs about going to strip clubs and sleeping with underage groupies). By the end of the 2000s, Pearl Jam had nothing left to prove. They were assured a base level of record sales, and that their fans would turn out for their concerts: where the real money is made. The only thing a new Pearl Jam record had to be, was *not* embarrassing. From this point on, the press greeted every new release with mild surprise that the band were still kicking, and reviewers noted with condescending fondness that the band could still write a decent tune.

And tunes are indeed what *Backspacer* delivers, in spades. This album continues the unpretentious audience-friendly approach of their self-titled album. The songs are all tight and punchy, and none of them outstays their welcome. Neither does the album: at 36:40 in length, it's Pearl Jam's shortest by a substantial margin. It rushes by in a whirlwind of positive vibes. Vedder told *Rolling Stone,* 'I've tried, over the years, to be hopeful in the lyrics, and I think that's going to be easier now'. The 2008 election of Barack Obama, inspired Vedder's more-optimistic outlook. The United States' first black president used as his campaign slogan, the single word 'Hope', and that feeling was certainly in the air when recording began.

But by the time *Backspacer* was released, the global financial crisis had hit, and things were looking grim again. It seemed like the band were playing it safe when they should be fired up. Some fans *hate* this album. In fan polls, it's regularly ranked near the bottom, below even *Binaural* and *Riot Act*. The most common criticism is that it's too slight, too one-note, and its overt positivity is somewhat gauche.

In terms of the wider musical landscape, if punters wanted *sad-bastard* music, they need only look elsewhere on the *Billboard* charts. By the turn of the 2000s, the biggest rock acts in the world were bands like My Chemical Romance, Fall Out Boy and Paramore: the *third wave* of emo. They combined punk energy with confessional songwriting and added some glam-rock drama and stadium theatricality. While someone like Mudhoney's Mark Arm would probably vomit blood at the idea that Fall Out Boy had anything in common with punk rock, 2000s emo was the last time rock-and-roll of any kind was the de facto music of moody teenagers and social outcasts. In that way, these bands served the same function as Pearl Jam once did.

The title *Backspacer* was inspired by Vedder's love of old typewriters. If there's a less punk-rock inspiration for an album title, I can't think of it. On the other hand, they also used the album title to name the turtle they sponsored in Conservation International and *National Geographic*'s 2009 Great Turtle Race: which is in keeping with their oceanic charity efforts.

The album artwork is among the band's best. It consists of ten surreal cartoon panels drawn by Dan Perkins aka Tom Tomorrow. As an editorial cartoonist, Perkins had lost income when Village Voice Media suspended all syndicated cartoons in 2009, so his friend Vedder hired him for this. The band set up an online game for fans to find the various panels hidden on other websites. When they found them all, they were able to download a demo of 'Speed Of Sound'. Those who bought the album on CD or through iTunes were also granted access to download two of nine pre-selected Pearl Jam concerts from 2005-2008. It was heartening to see Pearl Jam embrace the internet in such a fan-friendly manner. They even made the entire album available to play in the *Rock Band* video game. Pearl Jam were still happy to try new ways to reach their audience.

*Backspacer* was released on Pearl Jam's own brand-new Monkeywrench Records label, and distributed via Universal Music in the US, and Island Records internationally. It topped the *Billboard* 200: their first album to do so since *No Code*. It also reached number 1 in Canada, Australia and New Zealand, and the top 10 around the world. It also sold 7000 vinyl copies, which was impressive back in 2009 when vinyl was only just beginning its sales resurgence. There were different bonus tracks included on different digital editions, to encourage buyers to use a particular online store: now a common practice. Amazon UK had a live version of 'Immortality', while Canadian iTunes had a live version of 'Better Man'.

## 'Gonna See My Friend' (Vedder)
The album kicks off with this short and satisfying rocker. The opening riff is similar to Sex Pistols' 'God Save The Queen', but with more of a peppy surf-rock feel. The best part is the chord change going into the chorus, when the twin guitars lock in and around the title refrain, 'I'm gonna see my friend/Make it go away'. On first blush, that chorus seems tinged with darkness; it sounds like the friend Vedder is referring to is a drug dealer. But he has clarified that the song is about trying to talk someone out of using drugs.

## 'Got Some' (Ament, Vedder)
This song maintains the album's high energy with a thundering drum pattern and a guitar riff like an air-raid siren. It's a dynamic song, moving from tense verses to a soaring chorus to a forceful bridge. But where there should be a solo, there's a slow dramatic breakdown where nothing interesting really happens. The lyrics continue the allusions to drug use, this time from the drug pusher's point of view. But what he's actually selling – according to a Vedder interview with *The Globe And Mail* – is a good old-fashioned rock song. 'Get it on before it's gone', he sings. Could Vedder tell that rock and roll's time as the default music of youth and rebellion was coming to an end?

## 'The Fixer' (Cameron, Gossard, McCready, Vedder)
This was the album's first single: a radio-friendly blast of positivity. There was a sense of optimism in the air after Obama's election, but Vedder knew there was still work to be done. This song is not a call to social action, but a call to oneself. The song's is that when things are bad, it's up to you to try to fix it. As Vedder roars on the chorus: 'Fight to get it back again'.

This might be the Pearl Jam song most indebted to classic rock. The opening riff is all Who-style power chords; the 'Yeah yeah yeah yeah' refrain can't help but remind one of The Beatles, and the little one-off keyboard flourish before the bridge sounds like something Journey would do. The music was mostly composed by Matt Cameron – by far his most traditional rock work for the band so far, and bless him for it.

This single reached 3 on the Alternative Rock radio charts, and no higher than 10 on any other chart globally. It deserved a lot better.

## 'Johnny Guitar' (Cameron, Gossard, Vedder)

The band must've put all their hooks into the first three tracks, leaving nothing for this pleasant but anonymous rocker. There isn't even a real chorus, just a wah-wah breakdown. Lyrically it's interesting, if a trifle clumsy. It's a character sketch inside another character sketch. Vedder – as the narrator – sings of his fascination with R&B legend Johnny 'Guitar' Watson and the beautiful models he's pictured with on his album covers. Vedder dreams that one of these women visits him, but she asks for Johnny instead. From this odd fantasy, one could possibly glean some insight into Vedder's psychology regarding fame, hero-worship, groupies, etc. But I wouldn't want to suppose.

## 'Just Breathe' (Vedder)

This was the album's second single and Pearl Jam's biggest hit since 'Last Kiss'. Astonishingly, it's their only original song to be certified platinum on any chart. That's largely due to downloads and streaming, meaning that Pearl Jam – alone among their 1990s brethren – managed to get a new song of theirs lodged in the collective consciousness of Gen-Z.

It's a tender song about accepting your lot in life and enjoying what you have. Some fans interpret it as a funeral song about learning to cope with loss and move on. But it's also a popular song for wedding ceremonies. It has the same simple beauty that Bob Dylan's 'Blowin' In The Wind' and Van Morrison's 'Into The Mystic' have: that it can mean different things to different people. With its uncomplicated guitar part and straightforward chord sequence, 'Just Breathe' sounds like a well-worn song. The keyboards have a thin childlike sound reminiscent of a recorder, and when the strings enter, it's like the 1960s folk revival.

This song is so charming and guileless that inevitably it's hated by much of the fan base. That's possibly due to the preponderance of mediocre cover versions on YouTube. For a certain crowd, 'Just Breathe' has become as infamous as Oasis' 'Wonderwall', for being the acoustic song that would-be balladeers threaten social gatherings with. However, in 2012 it was also covered by no less an American icon than Willie Nelson himself. Forget a Grammy – that cover is the highest honour Pearl Jam could ever receive.

## 'Amongst The Waves' (Gossard, Vedder)

This was the album's third single, and it's Vedder's most unabashed hymn to surfing and its therapeutic power. It's so unabashed that it feels rude to critique it. But in my opinion, the band didn't fully realise the material's potential. The chorus has a sense of grandeur baked into it, but it's not elevated by the music underneath. The song could've benefitted from a more-dynamic melody, with the music rising and falling across a greater range to make the chorus really leap out. The big emotional outpouring comes from McCready's guitar solo: a lovely little patchwork of short, punchy phrases.

## 'Unthought Known' (Vedder)

The title comes from British psychoanalyst Christopher Bollas, who coined the term to refer to experiences that influence our behaviour even when we don't have the mental tools to think about them consciously. This awkward title hides a strong song that sounds as if it could've come from *Yield*. The simple staccato riff is reminiscent of 'Wishlist', while the melody and the way it builds is similar to 'Faithless' or 'In Hiding'. The pounding piano enters just as Vedder unleashes his full voice, then the whole band kicks in and the effect is stunning.

In the lyric, Vedder recalls the feeling of a particularly beautiful evening sky over New York City's Central Park. He includes a lot of amorphous new-age remarks like 'Feel the path of every day' and 'Fill the air up with love'. But then the bridge is just the ominous refrain of 'Nothing left, nothing there, nothing here', repeated over and over. The lyric is a mishmash of positive and negative images, which arguably enables the song to capture the indescribable feeling of an experience that speaks directly to our unconscious.

## 'Supersonic' (Gossard, Vedder)

If you're going to steal the title of one of Oasis' greatest hits, then you need to come up with a more-memorable song than this. It's a fairly superficial up-and-at-'em kind of song. It is the album's hardest rocker, though it's about as hard as the Ramones' bubblegum punk – which is no bad thing. The chorus is undeniably fun, and the guitar breakdown and solo is one of the album's best moments, even if it's over in a flash.

## 'Speed Of Sound' (Vedder)

From the dramatic opening reminiscent of dramatic Elton John ballads such as 'I Guess That's Why They Call It The Blues', to the harmonised vocals, to the use of piano, organ, and castanets, it feels like they've over-seasoned this song. It reminds me less of the innocent beauty of *Pet Sounds* and more of the self-conscious Brian Wilson-isms of Wilco's *Summerteeth*. It's a song of resignation and regret, but for what? Vedder sings about the need to forgive himself and find inner peace, but the ultimate subject remains elusive. 'This night has been a long one/Waiting on a word that never comes'. Like 'The End', this may be about missing loved ones.

## 'Force Of Nature' (McCready, Vedder)

Beefy power chords and wah-wah licks promise a better song than they deliver. It's not bad, just aggressively unmemorable. The climactic guitar solo is especially lacking in character: just a succession of runs with no feeling to them. During the second verse there's a seesawing keyboard part that's wasted by being buried in the mix. The lyrics are better than the music – using storm and ocean metaphors to describe the emotional toll of being the partner of someone with demons.

## 'The End' (Vedder)

That's an appropriate title for an album's final song. And it's a very *final*-sounding song. If the band had broken up after this album, fans would've looked at these lyrics as an obvious sign of it coming:

> Cause friends they come and go
> People change, as does everything
> I wanted to grow old
> I just want to grow old

Acknowledging one's own age can be a sign that an artist is ready to retire. But later in the song, Vedder seems to long for someone to come and help him out of his funk: 'Before I disappear, whisper in my ear'. The key lines are 'How it pains to leave you here with the kids on your own/Just don't let me go'. Assuming he's not singing in character here, this is Vedder trying to reconcile his life as a touring musician with his love for his wife and children.

Fittingly, he gives the album's best vocal performance – perhaps his best in years, at least in terms of sounding as if he's singing straight from the heart with no pretence or self-consciousness. His voice has all its force and power, and yet it frequently sounds as if it's on the verge of cracking. The musical backing includes a string quartet and horns, accentuating the heartache without straying into easy-listening schmaltz. The abrupt ending is dramatic, but such a subdued climax short-changes this quite wonderful album.

# Pearl Jam Twenty (2011)

Personnel:
Dave Abbruzzese: drums
Jeff Ament: bass
Matt Cameron, Jack Irons, Dave Krusen: drums
Stone Gossard, Mike McCready: guitar
Eddie Vedder: lead vocals
Producer: Pearl Jam
Recorded 1990-2010
Release date: 19 September 2011
Chart places: US: 15, UK: 91
Running time: 128:06

To celebrate their 20th anniversary, Pearl Jam released a documentary covering their entire career, and this identically titled companion compilation of live tracks, demos, and odds and ends from the film. The documentary was directed by Cameron Crowe, who made *Singles* and was executive producer of Pearl Jam's 1998 VHS documentary *Single Video Theory*. Crowe also wrote the *Pearl Jam Twenty* liner notes. His involvement bestowed a degree of prestige on this project. It was one thing appearing in a 1992 rom-com by Cameron Crowe: the writer of teen comedies *Fast Times At Ridgemont High* and *Say Anything*; it was another thing to have a whole film made about them by Cameron Crowe the Oscar-winning writer/director of *Jerry Maguire* and *Almost Famous*.

The film will convert sceptics who still have the band pegged as mopey young whippersnappers. The same can't be said for this compilation, as it's the very definition of a fan-only release. While there are historical curios and insights into the band's working methods, it's not a very cohesive listening experience. The sound quality of the live tracks varies wildly, and the demos are only worth listening to once.

The all-live first disc opens with a nice version of 'Release' from 2006, goes back to a 1990 performance of 'Alive', and proceeds chronologically up until 'Just Breathe' from 2010. The early recordings of 'Alive', 'Garden' and 'Why Go' are sub-bootleg quality, but they capture the raw energy of this fledgling band playing in small venues. 'Black' is from the *MTV Unplugged* concert, which was the only legal way to own a recording from that until the 2009 *Ten* reissue. The best live cut is undoubtedly 'Not for You', on which the guitarists excel. There are two covers – 'Walk with Me' is a lesser Neil Young song from his 2010 album *Le Noise*, recorded with Young at his Bridge School concert. 'Crown Of Thorns' is a cover of the Mother Love Bone song: recorded at Pearl Jam's 10th-anniversary show in Las Vegas on 22 October 2000. This was the first time they played it, and the performance is a touching tribute to Andrew Wood.

The second disc contains some interesting demos. Chris Cornell's original demo of 'Say Hello 2 Heaven' is powerful enough that the sound quality doesn't matter. The demo of 'Times Of Trouble' is the one from the tape that Jack Irons gave to Vedder, and is magical. Ament's 'Nothing As It Seems' demo is pretty good, but the live version that follows, shows how the band turned it into an epic. McCready's 'Given to Fly' and Cameron's 'Need To Know' (which became 'The Fixer') both show how inspiration is captured. The other original *songs* on this collection are instrumental scraps that never became full songs – 'Acoustic #1', 'It Ain't Like That', and the gentle McCready piece 'Be Like Wind' that was part of the film score.

Except for a lovely instrumental edit of 'Of The Girl', the remainder of the second disc is live tracks. 'Indifference' – with the audience singing and clapping along – is terrific. The soundcheck recording of 'Faithful' is also something special. So too is 'Bu$hleaguer', but for a different reason: you can hear the crowd's displeasure at the song. Bravo to the band for including it. The compilation concludes with two of Pearl Jam's biggest anthems: 'Rearviewmirror' and 'Better Man'. The audience participation on the latter – with its extended call-and-response coda – demonstrates the communal relationship Pearl Jam has with their audience. This track – along with 'Black' and 'Crown Of Thorns' – is worth owning this compilation for if you don't want to splash out on the complete concerts that they came from.

# Lightning Bolt (2013)

Personnel:
Jeff Ament: bass
Matt Cameron: drums, backing vocals
Stone Gossard: guitar, bongos
Mike McCready: guitar, bass
Eddie Vedder: lead vocals, guitar, ukulele
With:
Boom Gasper: piano, keyboards
Brendan O'Brien: piano
Ann Marie Calhoun: strings
Producer: Brendan O'Brien
Recorded at Henson Studios, Los Angeles, California; Studio X, Seattle,
Washington, 2011-2013
Release date: 15 October 2013
Chart places: US: 1, UK: 2
Running time: 47:14

What was the state of rock in 2013? Well, the biggest music stories of the year were
the returns of David Bowie and Black Sabbath, and the death of Lou Reed. There
was plenty of great new rock music being made by hungry young artists, but they
had little chance of reaching a mass audience. By now, the forces of pop, hip hop
and dance music had – with the aid of corporate sponsors, social media managers
and music-and-video streaming algorithms – merged into an unstoppable
commercial monoculture. The wider pop-culture landscape had no more bearing
on what Pearl Jam got up to than the movements of the stars did, and vice versa.

The band started recording new songs with Brendan O'Brien during the
preparations for *Twenty*, and they released the non-album single 'Olé' in 2011
(see Extras). They weren't entirely happy with the material they recorded, so
they focused on side projects for most of 2012, before regrouping in 2013 to
finish the album. It was a low-stakes no-pressure situation, and the result was
the previously unthinkable: an utterly bland Pearl Jam album, worthy of neither
condemnation nor acclamation.

*Lightning Bolt* is the first Pearl Jam album that feels like it exists only for the
sake of having a new Pearl Jam album out. It doesn't feel as if the band have
anything of great personal significance to say. And that's fine! Not every album
has to be *Plastic Ono Band* or *In Utero*. There's nothing wrong with making
straightforward rock music for the sake of it. It's just that this music is a little
*too* straight. It's the sound of Pearl Jam going through the motions, pulling off
the moves they can do in their sleep. You can't really blame them for that; after
all, they had just celebrated their 20th anniversary. I just wish this album was
more of a victory lap than a pleasant jog.

Even the cover is ordinary. It looks more like a modern minimalist brand
logo than an album cover. The booklet illustrations are more interesting. All

the art was done by Don Pendleton, who made designs for skateboards; one can imagine these clear-cut archetypal images working well in that format. The album won a Grammy for Best Recording Package, which is another sign that rock was in decline.

I may be in the minority in being disappointed by this album. It generally received good reviews, and fans regard it as an improvement on *Backspacer*. It debuted at number 1 on the charts in the US, Canada and Australia. At number 2 in the UK, it was also their highest-charting album there since *Vs.*. This may reflect less on the album's quality and more on the overall decline in album sales since the advent of streaming. Pearl Jam's fans are the type who still buy physical albums, while artists that are exponentially more popular on Spotify and YouTube, didn't register on the charts in 2013. (*Billboard* updated their chart tracking to account for streaming in 2014.) The band again used an unconventional tactic to get their music heard by the masses – by licensing the entire album and 36 other songs to Fox Sports for their coverage of the 2013 baseball World Series.

### 'Getaway' (Vedder)
The album kicks into gear immediately with a stomping rhythm and aggressive riffing. There's nothing particularly memorable about the music or the melody, but it does have a lot of energy. The best moment is when the guitars cut out for the start of the second verse, and there's just Vedder hollering over the drums. There's also a solid guitar solo consisting of a succession of short phrases. Lyrically, it initially seems like Vedder is having a go at critics of the band's musical stagnation: 'Everyone's a critic looking back up the river', followed by 'I found my place and it's alright'. But then it turns into a treatise on religious intransigence. So, nothing new here then.

### 'Mind Your Manners' (McCready, Vedder)
This was the album's first single, and at only 2:38 in length, it's Pearl Jam's shortest single to date. It's a neat little song, with a bare-bones rat-a-tat riff, a wailing solo, and another lyrical screed against organised religion. As a taster for the album, this felt like they were trying a little too hard to assert their punk credentials, by doing a Dead Kennedys impression. This isn't the same as when they released 'Spin The Black Circle' to preview *Vitalogy*; back then they had the world's attention, and choosing that as a lead single actually made a statement. This choice of single felt like the band were desperate to not be labelled a heritage act, which is pointless, since, in the 21st century, any band that can last more than three albums in the face of the public's overwhelming indifference to all things rock, is branded a heritage act by default. In 2013, there was a whiff of *How do you do, fellow kids?* about this song.

### 'My Father's Son' (Ament, Vedder)
This is the third full-tilt rocker in a row, and it comes the closest to sounding like something from their 1990s albums – with its gloomy minor chords

juxtaposed against a bright major-chord bridge, and the lyrics about the son of a psychopath worrying if he's inherited a predisposition for evil. The most notable musical element is the fat bass sound, which makes sense, since Ament wrote the music. However, the album's six-string bass is actually played by McCready! The reverb-drenched guitar licks sound like they could've come from a Cure record, and it makes one wonder what Pearl Jam could do if they tried for a full-on goth rock sound.

## 'Sirens' (McCready, Vedder)

This was the album's second single, and a clear-cut attempt at rock-radio dominance. It hearkens back to Temple of The Dog in sounding like an earnest folk rock ballad that's been beefed up to arena size. With the reverberating guitar wailing in the distance, the music resembles Kings of Leon – one of the bands that could claim with some degree of credibility to have taken Pearl Jam's place as the mainstream roots-rock band *de jour*.

The problem with this song is that it sounds too calculated. From the get-go, the music is in fourth gear. So, when it switches up to fifth gear, it's not as if it takes a giant emotional leap, it just gets slightly louder. The lyric's theme of love giving you strength is likewise rather rote. All that said, the track *does* include the album's best guitar solo. McCready was inspired to write the music after attending a Roger Waters concert, and his solo has dramatic high notes reminiscent of David Gilmour – though this time in cosy solo-album mode rather than tortured Pink Floyd mode: à la McCready's playing on 'Nothing As It Seems'.

## 'Lightning Bolt' (Vedder)

Astonishingly, no Pearl Jam album up until this has had a title track! It's inexplicable that they chose to finally bestow that honour upon this song, as it's another undistinguished song about a woman who is like a force of nature. It gets more interesting as it goes along, and it fades away on a motif that's more memorable than the track's other 80%.

## 'Infallible' (Ament, Gossard, Vedder)

Finally, something a little different. This song is built around a huge stomping drum rhythm and a squelchy keyboard riff. Interest quickly wanes, however, as the tune fails to go anywhere interesting. Even the solo sounds half-hearted. Lyrically, it's another lament about the state of the world – in this case, how humanity ignores oncoming disasters until it's too late. They would delve more into this topic on their next album.

## 'Pendulum' (Ament, Gossard, Vedder)

This song feels out of place on this album, and indeed it was composed during the *Backspacer* sessions. It's this album's most experimental track, relatively speaking. The use of bongos and bells make this sound like a goth Santana.

(That's not a criticism.) The twangy guitar solo is right out of a western movie soundtrack: something by Ry Cooder perhaps. If only the vague existential lyrics were as interesting.

## 'Swallowed Whole' (Vedder)

This kicks off with an urgent two-note acoustic guitar riff, sounding like one of the faster songs on Bruce Springsteen's *Nebraska*. That feeling lasts for a few bars before the rest of the band come in and it becomes yet another mid-tempo melodic rocker. There's nothing here that, say, Matchbox 20 or Live couldn't have managed. Lyrically, it's another ode to surfing, but without the cathartic ambition of 'Among the Waves'.

## 'Let The Record Play' (Gossard, Vedder)

This is the album's one true wild card, in the sense that it sounds like the band are finally having some wild fun. Ironically, it stands out by reverting to the most overworked sound in all of rock and roll: the 12-bar-blues boogie. The swinging beat and lashing of heavy guitar make this a worthy tribute to the power of vinyl. It's not too dissimilar to *Fandango*-era ZZ Top, which is never an insult. It's a pity they couldn't have come up with a better vocal hook, since blues rock was briefly back in vogue in 2013 thanks to bands like The Black Keys and Cage the Elephant. With a little more work, this could've been a radio hit.

## 'Sleeping By Myself' (Vedder)

This is a remake of a song from Vedder's 2011 solo album *Ukulele Songs*: which explains that instrument's presence here. It's an extremely likeable song, but the band members' contributions don't especially improve it. The original had more of a charming homemade feel, which compensates somewhat for the self-pitying lyrics.

## 'Yellow Moon' (Ament, Vedder)

This inscrutable song shares its title (and unfortunately nothing else) with the excellent 1989 Neville Brothers album. As if my complaint about the previous song was heard, this song is stripped down to the bare essentials – letting the instruments ring out and the melody breathe, and it's all the better for it. The song seems to have barely begun before a lovely guitar solo enters and leaves.

## 'Future Days' (Vedder)

This is the album's best song and is by far one of the most emotionally-affecting Vedder has ever written. It's about the loss of his friend Dennis Flemion, who drowned in 2012. 'If I ever lose you/I would surely lose myself', Vedder sings. Piano, acoustic guitar, strings and keyboards are all used judiciously for maximum effect. The relative simplicity reminds me of another neglected late-period album closer by a great American artist: 'And So It Goes' by Billy Joel.

'Future Days' gained prominence after it was featured in the video game *The Last Of Us, Part II*, sung in-universe by the game's father figure to his adoptive daughter. If you know the plot of the game, you'll understand how effective this song is in context.

# Gigaton (2020)

Personnel:
Jeff Ament: bass, guitar, keyboards, piano, drum programming
Matt Cameron: drums, drum programming, guitar, backing vocals
Stone Gossard: guitar, bass, percussion, keyboards, backing vocals
Mike McCready: guitar, percussion, keyboards
Eddie Vedder: lead vocals, guitar, keyboards, pump organ
With:
Josh Evans: keyboards, drum programming
Brendan O'Brien: keyboards
Meagan Grandall: backing vocals
Producer: Josh Evans
Recorded at Pearl Jam's custom studio, Seattle, Washington, 2017-2020
Release date: 27 March 2020
Chart places: US: 5, UK: 6
Running time: 57:03

For most of pop music history – and especially during the early-1990s CD boom, it was expected that artists would release a new album every two or three years at least. Waiting any longer could doom you to irrelevancy as you were overtaken by a new musical fad, or worse, by your own imitators. Nowadays, it's not unusual for rock acts to take four or five years between albums. For indie artists, that's likely because it's hard to make a living from music these days – physical sales have bottomed out, streaming royalties are negligible, and touring can be cost-prohibitive. For big-selling legacy artists, it is much the same. Why work your butt off to make new music that won't earn you any money and will be overshadowed by your old hits played over and over on corporate-mandated radio playlists?

So, Pearl Jam taking more time between albums was expected. But seven years? Nirvana's entire career could fit in the time between *Lightning Bolt* and *Gigaton*. Pearl Jam did release a Brandi Carlile cover in 2017, and the non-album single 'Can't Deny Me' in 2018 (see Extras). The latter was advertised as being from an upcoming album, but it took another two years for that album to arrive, and that song was deemed surplus to requirements.

Fortunately, the long wait for *Gigaton* was worth it. Pearl Jam's 11th album is their most sonically eclectic since *Riot Act*, and their most successful balance of eclecticism and songwriting since *Yield*. Beginning with the self-titled 2006 album, critics declared every Pearl Jam album as 'their best since the 1990s', but this is the one album for which that claim does not seem like hot air. I should avoid overhyping it myself; this is still very much a straightforward rock album. But there's a freshness to the songwriting and playing here that the preceding albums lacked.

Part of that freshness can be attributed to a new producer. Josh Evans had worked as a studio assistant and technician for the band since 2004, and they appointed him to oversee building their custom Seattle studio. When it became operational in 2017, the band employed Evans to co-produce their new music. He'd previously worked on side projects by Ament and McCready, and also Soundgarden's successful 2012 reunion album *King Animal.* He'd also worked for Chris Cornell as a monitor engineer on the 2016 Temple Of The Dog tour, and as a guitar tech on Soundgarden's reunion tour.

The Chris Cornell connection was especially significant for a tragic reason. In 2017, Cornell – the man whose project to honour his fallen friend had helped bring Pearl Jam together – died by suicide. This was a horrifying shock to everyone, including Pearl Jam. Cornell was revered by his fans and peers, and at the time, he seemed to be on the crest of another career resurgence. While initial reports blamed drugs, it was known that he suffered from depression and intrusive thoughts. His death is another reminder that just because you're rich and admired, it doesn't mean all your psychological wounds are magically healed. This theme has been a constant throughout Pearl Jam's career.

However, Cornell's death isn't directly referenced on this album. It's just one of the many depressing real-world events that formed a backdrop to the album – along with the threat of climate change, and the United States government's swing back to the right. Four years after Donald Trump's election, one could've expected a politically engaged band like Pearl Jam to devote a fair amount of disc space to talking about him, but aside from a few references, they do not. The album's dominant theme is the environment. That comes across most overtly in the album art, which is atypically classicist for Pearl Jam. It's a Paul Nicken photo of a polar ice cap in the process of melting. On the album's physical edition – with its metallic sheen – the image is particularly striking. The artwork was the centrepiece of the album's promotional teaser campaign: a virtual scavenger hunt. Visiting an interactive map of the band's website, led fans to find billboards in cities around the world that when viewed through a particular Instagram filter, played snippets of new songs and showed an animation of ice caps melting. As a promotional stunt, that's less *rock and roll* than, say, Queen's army of nude bicyclists, but possibly more educational. The album title comes from the use of the unit gigaton to measure the rate of melting ice caps.

*Gigaton* was released to effusive reviews and the band's lowest chart placings since *Riot Act* in 2002. *C'est la vie.* The band had produced an album of which they could be proud. It would've undoubtedly sold more if they'd been able to tour it immediately, as they had planned. However, the COVID-19 pandemic hit the US in the months leading up to the album's release, so the band pushed their world tour back to 2021, and then again to 2022. They *did* play some US festival dates in late-2021, where they unveiled Josh Klinghoffer as their new additional touring guitarist. Klinghoffer is another ex-Red Hot Chili Peppers member, and his playing should bring new dimensions to Pearl Jam's songs. The future looks bright for the band everyone expected to burn out.

## 'Who Ever Said' (Vedder)

Is this U2? The album fades in on a burbling synth line reminiscent of one of the Irish band's more ambitious albums, like *Zooropa*. But before it gets too artsy, the intro is abruptly cut off by a nicely grinding riff. There's more space between the instruments on this album, giving the music a wide-open-sky feel. There's a looseness to this song's playing, as if the band were willing to let this music breath, rather than try and cram it into a preconceived form.

This song has an unusual sprawling structure. After the first verse and chorus, there's an instrumental break and then another chorus. After that, it slows down for some instrumental noodling, and then what seems like a middle eight becomes the main melody. From there on, the song builds up, faster and more furious, until the chorus explodes again with the line 'Whoever said it's all been said, gave up on satisfaction'. That could be this album's statement of purpose: don't count this band out, because they still have something to say.

## 'Superblood Wolfmoon' (Vedder)

Released as another album taster, this was more in line with what people expected of Pearl Jam than the first single was. The title is strangely endearing in its ridiculousness, as are the lyrics. Vedder sings about the end of a relationship, with some beautifully overwrought language: 'She was a stunner and I am stunned'; 'Throughout the hopelessness, focus on your focusness'. This is the kind of song that seems more absurd the more you dissect it. But because it's pulled off with such panache, it's difficult to dislike. The downward guitar shredding going into the solo is incredible, and the solo itself is a full-on Eddie Van Halen-style freak-out.

## 'Dance Of The Clairvoyants' (Ament, Cameron, Gossard, McCready, Vedder)

I don't think anyone was expecting this. When Pearl Jam announced the first single from their new album, most assumed that the best-case scenario was a slight improvement on 'Mind Your Manners'. What we got instead was a full-on homage to Talking Heads: a band about as far from Pearl Jam's usual sound and style as any band could possibly be. This song should be an embarrassment, but in fact, it's near genius. It even incorporates some electronic elements to bring it more in line with the modern bands that Talking Heads inspired, like LCD Soundsystem.

The robotic drum pattern is a looped sample of Matt Cameron's playing, while the surging bass riff is played by Gossard. Ament instead plays the burbling keyboards that give the song its retro-futurist feel. Vedder starts singing in his normal manner, but when the Nile Rodgers-style funk guitar enters, all bets are off. Vedder mimics David Byrne's kooky vocal delivery when he growls out 'Save your prrredictions, burn your assumptions', and he replicates Byrne's wordplay-based lyric style with lines like 'It's not a negative thought/I'm positive/Positive'. What is he positive of? – that we need to get out of our own way and stop expecting things to be perfect.

The chorus is perhaps not as strong as the music deserves – it slows down and gets meditative just when the dance should be heating up. But the fade-out – with Vedder singing 'Stand back when the spirit comes' while he also wails in the background like a lost shaman – is transcendent. This song should be an absolute stunner, live.

The single release was supported with *three* videos: the last of which is the *official* one. But they all consist of similar nature footage. This single was not a big hit, but it certainly piqued the interest of those who might've written off new Pearl Jam music.

## 'Quick Escape' (Ament, Vedder)

This song is a mix of classic-rock influences. The John Bonham-esque drum rhythm and grinding bass/guitar riff à la Led Zeppelin's 'The Wanton Song', are the closest Pearl Jam have come to sounding like them since *Vs.*. The first guitar solo – a searing sheet of noise – could be The Edge, while the second solo is pure Hendrix. Ament's bass goes into overdrive near the end, leaving us with a taster of what a proper bass solo from him might be like.

This is the album's only song to explicitly name-check Trump. One line says they had to travel the world 'to find a place Trump hadn't fucked up yet'. But Vedder is not speaking of the real world: the song is a reflection from a fantastical future place where the remnants of humanity fled to after having messed-up Earth.

This was released as the album's third single, two days before *Gigaton* itself. It's the most radio-appropriate of the album's singles, but the lyric content probably put paid to any substantial airtime. It's another song that should absolutely *slay* live.

## 'Alright' (Ament)

The album's first ballad is based around a twinkling six-note motif that could've come from an early-1980s British synth-pop record. It isn't a synthesizer though, but an African percussion instrument called a Mbira. That instrument and ghostly guitar washes add a sense of the mystery to what is a pleasant but rote ballad. The lyric's message is that one should not be afraid to be alone, to keep part of oneself shielded from the world. It's the same theme Vedder has been harping on since *Vitalogy*, but here it's delivered with more equanimity.

## 'Seven O'Clock' (Ament, Gossard, McCready, Vedder)

In terms of length, subject matter and its placement in the tracklist, this is the album's centrepiece. It's the most overtly political song on the album, even if it doesn't name names. Written in blank verse, at first it seems like a call-to-action to fix the world: 'This fucked up situation calls for all hands on deck', 'Freedom is as freedom does'. But as the song goes on, it takes on a more rueful tone and seems to be about a social activist reflecting on better days and lamenting that there's still so much work to be done. As befits the subject matter, the melody is strident, and the pace is martial.

This song was pieced together from different portions of a jam session, and it's a credit to Evans' skill that it sounds all of one piece. Waves of effect-laden Pink Floyd-style guitars, rise and fall throughout. The chorus swells on a bed of keyboards that sound vaguely Celtic. Strip away the vocals, and this could be part of a film score, played during the triumphant final game for the retiring baseball legend, or something like that. At around four minutes in, there's a dramatic key change, and the music swells to bursting in a triumphant way: a trick well used by the likes of U2, R.E.M. and, more recently, Coldplay. Vedder's keening on the outro is very much the sort of thing Michael Stipe did.

### 'Never Destination' (Vedder)
This is the album's first nondescript song. It's a perfectly fine rocker with a very good guitar solo. But it wouldn't lose anything from being half as long. Lyrically, it appears to be about wanderlust. But there are also allusions to surfing, which here sounds dangerous rather than spiritual. There are also references to novelist Paul Theroux, and Bob Honey: a character from the novel *Bob Honey Who Just Do Stuff* by Sean Penn (the director of *Into The Wild,* which Vedder wrote the music for).

### 'Take The Long Way' (Cameron)
This is the most aggressive track thus far, thanks to the growling guitar riff. With its stop/start rhythms and woozy chorus, it is, of course, the work of Matt Cameron. While it's not anything exceptional, it's comforting to know that 30 years into their career the band are as collectively locked in as they are on this track. Again, the wild guitar-soloing makes the song worth it. There are also female backing vocals for the first time on a Pearl Jam album: from Seattle singer-songwriter Meagan Grandall.

### 'Buckle Up' (Gossard)
If ever a title should've been used for an opening track, it's this one. But this song would not have been suited to such a placement. It's a folk rock tune with a bouncy riff and a marching pace, similar to R.E.M.'s 'We Walk'. The chorus sounds more like a lullaby than a promise of impending excitement. It's quite lovely, as long as you don't read the lyrics, which seem to be about a matricide!

### 'Comes Then Goes' (Vedder)
Now we're in classic 1970s singer-songwriter territory: just Vedder alone with his acoustic guitar. This was apparently the song's first take. This plays to Vedder's strengths: a strong melody backed by forceful close-mic'ed strumming, allowing his voice to resonate. He sings of how anger, pain and sadness come and go, leaving questions in their wake. The message doesn't

entirely come together, but the feel is guileless and spontaneous enough to compensate. It is perhaps a little too long though. The album's last three songs are all five-six minutes long, which means that even with quality songs, the album's energy flags as it winds down.

## 'Retrograde' (McCready, Vedder)

This is another lengthy ballad, but this time the whole band is on board to keep it interesting. The layers of keyboards give it an otherworldly feel, sort of like Radiohead did when they weren't trying to pretend they weren't a rock band, viz., 'How To Disappear Completely'. The music stays grounded, though. It seems like it's building to a huge guitar solo, but that's not on the cards. I wouldn't complain, except the song also lacks a strong chorus hook. Ultimately, it's a good melody in search of a song. It dissolves into a morass of pleasant noise by the end: again, very similar to Radiohead.

The lyric is packed with nature metaphors and spiritual symbolism. It's vague enough to be interpreted in many ways, but its video clip featuring teenage activist Greta Thunberg makes it clear this is about climate change. The clip – a mixture of live-action and animation – combines the depiction of a climate apocalypse with tarot-card symbolism. It's an impressive video, if only because it was completed during the COVID-19 pandemic.

## 'River Cross' (Vedder)

This is another great closing song, about the need to keep moving ahead; to keep reaching for that dream; to imagine that there is even going to be a future. The title could be an allusion to Jimmy Cliff's classic reggae ballad 'Many Rivers to Cross', but the songs aren't similar. This song is all soft billowy keyboards, with the occasional drum shot ringing out. The pump organ was held over from Vedder's original demo.

The album ends with Vedder declaring that the forces arraying against humanity 'Won't hold us down'. If Pearl Jam never record another album, that's an appropriate sentiment for them to end on. But why should that be? Gigaton proves they have the creative power left for many more recordings.

## Extras

These are officially released studio recordings by Pearl Jam that are available on singles, compilations and soundtracks, but which haven't been included on a Pearl Jam album. Live covers and non-album live tracks are excluded since a complete record of Pearl Jam's live material would fill a whole other book!

## 'I Got A Feeling'

This was included as a bonus track on the original Japanese edition of *Ten*. It's a cover of the Lennon/McCartney song from The Beatles' final album, *Let It Be*. It's interesting that Pearl Jam's first-released cover wasn't a hardcore punk song or a stadium rock anthem but was an upbeat pop-soul album track. It demonstrated that the band's roots go deeper than their expected influences. Vedder sings both John and Paul parts: sometimes so forcefully it sounds like the microphone is about to short out. He ad-libs some lyrics about the notorious fake band Milli Vanilli. There are also uncredited backing vocals, presumably by Gossard.

## 'Real Thing' (Abbruzzese, Ament, Gossard, Freese, Muggard, Reyes)

This is from the soundtrack to the 1993 film *Judgement Night*. That soundtrack is more well-known than its film, because it was one of the first and most successful experiments in mixing rock and hip hop, long before nu metal turned that idea into a pandering joke. Every song on the soundtrack is a collaboration between a hip hop artist and an alternative or heavy metal band. Most of the pairings work extremely well because each band was paired with a rapper of comparable hardness. Whoever decided to pair Mudhoney and Sir Mix-a-Lot, deserves a raise!

Pearl Jam's collaboration with West Coast group Cypress Hill, is fun, but not one of the album's highlights. It sounds like an instrumental demo that was handed to the other group to rap over. Vedder is not even heard except for some wordless vocals during the bridge and coda. Cypress Hill – and particularly B-Real's nasal voice – are an acquired taste, but their rapping on this can't be faulted. This soundtrack is worth owning, but not really for this song.

## 'Catholic Boy' (Carroll)

This is from the 1995 movie *The Basketball Diaries*. It's a cover of a 1980 song by Jim Carroll, who wrote the book the film is based on. Carroll sings this song with Pearl Jam backing him. It's a great performance of a solid but unexceptional traditional punk song. What's most notable, is the contrast between the band's grungy modern-rock performance and Carroll's nervy new wave vocals.

## 'Out Of My Mind' (Abbruzzese, Ament, Gossard, McCready, Vedder)

This live improvisation was the B-side of the 'Not For You' single. It's one of only two original Pearl Jam B-sides not included on *Lost Dogs*: which is annoying, because there was space on the CDs for this and 'Leatherman'. This is a perfectly enjoyable piece of swamp rock, that brings the band's Creedence Clearwater Revival influence to the fore.

## 'Leatherman' (Vedder)

Given the jittery new wave sound of this 'Given To Fly' B-side, you'd assume it was about someone like Lou Reed or Iggy Pop. But actually, it was inspired by the urban legend of an unidentified 1880s New York vagabond. This is better than many songs that *were* included on *Lost Dogs*, so it's a shame this wasn't.

## 'Soldier Of Love' (Buzz Carson, Tony Moon)

This was released on the same 1998 fan-club single as 'Last Kiss', and was included along with that song on the 1999 *No Boundaries* charity compilation. Overshadowed by its far-more-famous comrade, this is a solid – if plodding – cover of a good song that was originally recorded by soul singer Arthur Alexander in 1962. The opening line 'Lay down your arms', jibes with the compilation album's cause, even if the rest of the song is a basic romantic entreaty; evidence – if such were needed – that Vedder could've been a successful 1960s crooner à la Scott Walker or Tom Jones.

## 'The Kids Are Alright' (Pete Townsend)

From the 2001 tribute album *Substitute: The Songs of The Who*, this is a live cover of The Who's greatest 1960s youth anthem that isn't 'My Generation'. Unfortunately, it's a fairly rote and workmanlike cover, with Vedder sounding particularly underpowered. The album it's from is one of the worst examples of a cut-rate cash-in tribute compilation. Much better is Pearl Jam's take on The Who's 'Baba O'Riley', which is a frequent concert closer.

## 'Master Of War' (Bob Dylan)

A live recording of this Bob Dylan protest classic was included on the soundtrack to Michael Moore's 2004 documentary *Fahrenheit 9/11*. It's fine, but Pearl Jam fans who are also Dylan fans should check out Vedder and McCready's performance of this song on the Bob Dylan *30th-Anniversary Concert Celebration* album. Not only is that a more intense performance from the younger and hungrier musicians, but it demonstrates they were able to hold their own amidst rock icons including Neil Young, Eric Clapton, George Harrison, Tom Petty, Roger McGuinn, Lou Reed, The Band, Willie Nelson, Kris Kristofferson, John Mellencamp, Stevie Wonder, and Dylan himself. As the token *young 'uns* in the lineup, they acquitted themselves admirably.

## 'Love Reign O'er Me' (Pete Townsend)

This song – the climax of 1973's *Quadrophenia* – is one of The Who's greatest songs, and their recording features a truly titanic vocal performance from Roger Daltrey. Vedder was understandably trepidatious about covering it, and you can tell he's giving it his absolute all. His voice sounds rougher and more strained than Daltrey's, but that adds to the drama. The band's performance is exemplary, and the use of real strings instead of synths like on The Who's original, gives this recording a cinematic feel. Fittingly, this was included on the soundtrack to the 2007 post-9/11 drama film *Reign Over Me*.

## 'Olé' (Ament, Vedder)

This non-album single was released to streaming services in 2011, to little fanfare. There is genuinely very little one can say about this song. It's a fast rocker without a memorable riff, melody or hook. Lyrically it seems to be about laughing in the face of oncoming doom. The only thing of note is the long and powerful string-bend going into the guitar solo.

### 'I Want You So Hard (Boys Bad News)' (Josh Homme, Jesse Hughes)

This is a cover of a song by retro-rock band Eagles Of Death Metal. During a concert by that band on 13 November 2015 at the Bataclan in Paris, Islamist terrorists attacked the audience, killing 89 people. One week later, Pearl Jam released this live cover of that band's best garage-rock thrasher, alongside Matt Cameron's synth-pop cover of the same band's song 'I Love You All the Time'. The single's sales went to Eagles of Death Metal member Josh Homme's charity Sweet Stuff Foundation, to support the victim's families.

### 'Again Today' (Brandi Carlile)

This is from the 2017 album *Cover Stories*, which is a complete cover of folk-rocker Brandi Carlile's 2007 album *The Story*. A host of roots-rock icons (plus Adele) cover a song each. It was released to raise money for the charity War Child UK. Why Brandi Carlile and why this album? Your guess is as good as mine. Pearl Jam transform this song from Carlile's delicate original into a full-bore rocker. Carlile's lyrics are close enough to Vedder's style, that you could mistake this for a Pearl Jam original. Interesting to note: in 2020, Carlile recorded two Soundgarden covers with that band's surviving members, for release as a Record Store Day promo single, and she didn't do a half-bad job.

### 'Can't Deny Me' (McCready, Vedder)

This non-album single was released in 2018 to streaming services. It was originally intended for *Gigaton,* but was ultimately left off that album, which took another two years to arrive. This is nothing special, although it is more memorable than 'Olé', thanks to a grinding stop/start riff and the use of cowbell, handclaps and cash register sounds. Lyrically it's a fairly generic protest song with nothing specific in its sights.

### 'Get It Back' (Cameron)

This non-album single is from the portentously titled compilation *Good Music To Avert The Collapse Of American Democracy, Volume 2*: for which a host of indie, alt-country and underground hip hop artists donated unreleased tracks to help raise money for the Voting Rights Lab (an American organisation fighting voter suppression). Despite the title, this is not some cry against electoral corruption, but rather a song of support for a missing loved one. Musically, it's a mid-tempo ballad with good dynamics, that fades out just when it should be really taking off.

# The Ten Club holiday singles

Almost every year from 1991 to 2017, Pearl Jam gifted members of their Ten Club with a 7" vinyl of otherwise-unavailable recordings from that year. Mostly these are live covers featuring special guest musicians, but there are a handful of original songs. Some of these recordings have been made available on *Lost Dogs* and other compilations (see Extras). You can listen to the most recent singles on streaming services. However, the original vinyls remain collector's items.

Here are write-ups for the otherwise-unavailable originals:

### 'Ramblings' (Uncredited)

From the 1991 single. This was recorded while Pearl Jam were on tour with Red Hot Chili Peppers (in fact, you can hear them playing in the background). This consists of an acoustic riff over which the Pearl Jam members introduce themselves and talk bollocks. It's cute but is the very definition of inessential.

### 'Ramblings Continued' (Uncredited)

From the 1992 single. This is a sonic montage of song clips, interview segments and spoken messages from the band. The Beatles, Jimi Hendrix and Monty Python are easy to spot, but you'll need to concentrate to figure out the other sources, and you won't want to do that unless you're one of those weirdos who considers 'Revolution 9' to be their favourite Beatles song.

### 'Angel' (Abbruzzese, Vedder)

From the 1993 single. Despite its short length, this acoustic ballad packs a lot in – a solid melody, glistening guitar-strumming, soaring backing vocals and an intriguing spiritual lyric that touches on the mind-body problem. This definitely should've been included on *Lost Dogs*.

### 'Ramblings aka Fuck Me In The Brian' (Uncredited)

Also from the 1993 single. 'Fuck Me in The Brian' is a song from Vedder's pre-Pearl Jam band Bad Radio, and it was played live only one time. This was recorded at a concert on 5 November 1993, during which some fans pelted the band with shoes. Vedder sounds utterly deranged as he screams and swears his way through the song, before stopping to taunt the shoeless fans. At first, he threatens to beat them up, and then decides it would be more fitting to donate the offending shoes to charity. That's rock 'n' roll for you!

### 'Olympic Platinum' (Nick Didia)

From the 1996 single. This is a spoof of a typical inspirational power ballad – penned by the band's engineer Nick Didia around the time of the Atlanta Olympic Games. The use of falsetto and doo-wop backing vocals, plus the spoken-word sections, make this the closest Pearl Jam have come to sounding like Frank Zappa. If you can do that and not embarrass yourself, it's quite an achievement. This is the band's best original comedy song by a mile, and it's worth tracking down.

### 'Happy When I'm Crying' (Irons)

From the 1997 single. Penned by Jack Irons, this song sounds like nothing else in Pearl Jam's catalogue. It includes a brief introduction spoken in Spanish, a haunting keyboard line, psychedelic guitar, vocal effects and layers of exotic percussion. This would not have fitted on *No Code* or *Yield*, but it should be more widely heard.

### 'Last Soldier' (McCready)

From the 2001 single. A very Neil Young-like acoustic folk song – complete with harmonica – about a soldier departing for war. This is a far-more-effective protest song than 'Bu$hleaguer'.

### 'Santa God' (Vedder)

From the 2007 single. At first glance, this song could simply be about a child's perception of Christmas: that Santa seems more important than Jesus. But the urgent music and Vedder's intense vocal, give it an edge. It could also be about the commercialisation of Christmas, and how parents use the threat of Santa's *naughty list,* to keep children in line.

### 'Santa Cruz' (Vedder)

From the 2009 single. The title isn't just a Christmas pun: it's about Vedder visiting that beach. It's a bouncy little folk rock number – the closest Pearl Jam have come to sounding like 1970s Laurel Canyon soft rock – would that they pursued this style more.

### 'Turning Mist' (McCready)

From the 2010 single. This lovelorn ballad was written and sung by McCready, and it turns out he has quite a lovely voice! – not a voice suited to Pearl Jam's usual fare, but terrific on a straightforward heartfelt roots rock song like this. His solo is also short and sweet.

### 'No Jeremy' (Ament, Vedder)

From the 2011 single. This is an interesting live arrangement of 'Jeremy' from 20 June 1995. It's more subdued and sinister, and forgoes most of the vocals for a long slow instrumental build. I can imagine the audience at the time was disappointed, but it's worthwhile having this alternative version available.

### 'Falling Down' (Uncredited)

Also from the 2011 single. This song was played only once, at the same concert where 'No Jeremy' was recorded. It's a plodding ramble that could possibly have been developed into a good song, but it doesn't feel like any great loss.

## 'Devil Doll' (Exene Cervenka, John Doe)

From the 2012 single. This is a collaboration between Vedder and the band X. They were one of the original Los Angeles punk bands, and their combination of garage rock, surf and Americana was an influence on the entire 1980s underground US rock scene. This is a fun punkabilly song about that old rock 'n' roll staple: the scarily powerful woman. Vedder's voice, blends surprisingly well with that of X frontwoman Exene Cervenka.

## 'Pendulumorphosis' (Ament, Gossard)

From the 2015 single. This instrumental is a reimagining of the Pearl Jam song 'Pendulum', for piano, keyboard and strings: all performed by Ament. It's quite lovely, and shows off the bassist's talents. It has been used to introduce Pearl Jam concerts, but it sounds more suited to the title sequence of a 1980s conspiracy thriller.

# Live albums

Pearl Jam went for most of their 1990s heyday without releasing a live album, and then they decided to flood the market! There are now more Pearl Jam live albums in circulation than anyone can listen to in one lifetime. These come in two types: the regular wide-release live albums, and the 'official bootlegs'. Between these, you might be stymied by too many options. Rest assured that if you grab any Pearl Jam live album, you're going to hear some good music. You should choose one that features songs you like or some interesting cover songs. If you want to narrow it down further, here's some more information.

## Live On Two Legs

This was compiled from performances on their 1998 *Yield* tour. It's generally considered a solid-if-unexceptional album, that fails to convey the band's spontaneous side, or their in-concert connection with their fans. After this, with a few exceptions, the band would opt to present full shows instead of compilations.

## Live at Benaroya Hall

This was recorded in 2003 and released to raise money for the Seattle charity YouthCare. It's a semi-acoustic affair, which made it stand out from the glut of official bootlegs they released over the preceding three years. While it is subdued and one-note, this set highlights some of Pearl Jam's underrated softer songs, including 'Of The Girl' and 'Around The Bend'. There's also a fun cover of the Shel Silverstein-penned Johnny Cash hit '25 Minutes To Go'.

## Live At Easy Street

This short sharp EP was recorded at the titular Seattle record store in 2005. It's refreshing to hear Pearl Jam playing in such an intimate space again, and the setlist is a cool mix of underrated Pearl Jam originals and punk covers.

## Live At the Gorge 05/06

If you buy only one Pearl Jam live album, it should probably be this mammoth seven-CD box set that includes three whole concerts – one from their 2005 tour, and two from successive nights on their 2006 tour: all recorded at the Gorge Amphitheatre in George, Washington. The band is in peak form. Almost all their biggest songs are included, there's an acoustic mini-set, and many of their most-performed covers are included. There's also surprisingly little overlap between the setlists. And of the songs that do appear twice or thrice, you can hear how the band never play them the same way.

## Live at Lollapalooza 2007

This iTunes exclusive live album is notable mainly for a cover of Pink Floyd's 'Another Brick In The Wall (Part II)' and a guest appearance by Ben Harper.

## Live On Ten Legs

This 2011 release is a sequel to the 1998 album, compiling performances from 2003 to 2010. The setlist does not overlap with its predecessor, so if you buy both, you'll have a solid live *greatest hits*. But just like its predecessor, this album sounds polished and professional, rather than inspired.

## Let's Play Two

This was recorded at Chicago's Wrigley Field during their 2016 tour, and was also released as a concert film. It's notable for including a performance of Vedder's solo single 'All the Way', which was released in 2008 as a tribute to the Chicago Cubs baseball team.

## MTV Unplugged

In 2019, the band released a limited-edition vinyl of this classic 1992 performance, as a Record Store Day exclusive. Then in 2020 they *finally* made it available on CD and via streaming, as it always should've been. This is simply a must-have for fans of the *original* Pearl Jam.

## Official Bootlegs

Pearl Jam had always been happy to allow amateur taping of their shows. But when they saw how much bootleggers were charging fans for low-quality recordings, they stepped in. Beginning in 2000, the band began making soundboard-quality recordings of almost every concert, available to purchase in plain cardboard sleeves. At first, these were shipped to stores (resulting, in 2001, in Pearl Jam having the most albums to debut at once on the *Billboard 200*!). The recordings of the 2003 tour were first made available through mail order. Then starting with their 2005 tours, they were made available only via digital download from their website, which obviously saves on packaging. Selected concerts are also available on streaming services.

This practice earned them comparisons to Grateful Dead, whose remarkably long-lasting fan base was maintained through tape trading. But these releases serve a different function to the Dead's endless well of archival live shows. Deadheads are happy to listen to a dozen different live shows to absorb all the minute distinctions between different performances of 'Dark Star' and 'Truckin'' – whereas Pearl Jam fans are more interested in being able to own complete recordings of the concerts they were at. Nowadays, many artists offer downloads of their concerts, including a certain Mr. Springsteen. It's good for the fans, the artists and the environment.

There are over 300 official bootlegs available at the moment. The performances vary in quality of course, but even the worst is pretty good. There are some that stand out from the pack. *10/22/00 – Las Vegas, Nevada* is their 10th-anniversary show, and includes their first performance of 'Crown of Thorns', and covers of Pink Floyd's 'Interstellar Overdrive', Elvis Presley's 'Can't Help Falling In Love' and The Who's 'Baba O'Riley'. *11/6/00 – Seattle,*

*Washington* was the final show of their *Binaural* tour. It's a homecoming show, is almost three hours long, and includes *two* Who covers and the first-and-only performance of 'Alive' on that tour. *7/11/03 – Mansfield, Massachusetts* is an even longer 47-song set (with a 12-song acoustic mini-set) that includes an almost perfect mix of hits and album cuts, and has Boom Gasper on keyboards.

# Videos

These are official Pearl Jam video releases that are widely available. There are many unofficial videos, so beware! One movie that needs to be mentioned – even though it's not entirely focused on Pearl Jam – is the 1996 Doug Pray documentary *Hype!*, which documents (and takes the mickey out of) the 1990s grunge explosion. Pearl Jam – along with almost every notable Seattle band – perform and are interviewed.

## Single Video Theory

This 45-minute documentary covers the making of *Yield*, and includes performances of songs from that album, plus interesting behind-the-scenes footage.

## Touring Band 2000

This documents the North American leg of their 2000 *Binaural* tour, and gives insight into the life of a major band on tour. There are technically three otherwise-unavailable Pearl Jam songs included: three instrumentals used to accompany montages of their European tour legs.

## Live At the Garden

This is a complete recording of their 8 July 2003 performance at Madison Square Garden in New York City. The footage is incredible, and a host of top-shelf guest stars appear in the main concert and also the bonus material. If you only buy one Pearl Jam DVD, make it this one.

## Imagine In Cornice

This is a relatively short concert film compiled from their 2007 shows in Italy.

## Pearl Jam Twenty

This is the aforementioned Cameron Crowe-directed documentary, where the focus is less on live performance and more on telling the band's story. If you only buy *two* Pearl Jam DVDs, this should be the other one.

## Let's Play Two

This is the video equivalent of the live album of the same name, recorded at the same 2016 shows. This is Pearl Jam firmly ensconced in *elder statesman* mode.

# Solo Albums & Side Projects

The members of Pearl Jam have a pathological need to produce music. That's the only thing that can explain the sheer volume of extracurricular work they've been involved in. Their guest appearances on other musicians' songs are too numerous to list here. What follows is a brief rundown of their most essential solo albums and side projects.

## Eddie Vedder

Such was Vedder's high profile, that it was considered a question of *when* – not *if* – he would release a solo album. When one finally arrived, it wasn't what anyone expected. *Into The Wild* (2007) is the score for the Sean Penn movie of the same name, which tells the true story of Chris McCandless – an American nomad who left behind his comfortable middle-class life, to explore the wilderness, and who died at age 24 in remote Alaska. The story's themes naturally appealed to Vedder, who recorded the score playing almost all the instruments himself. The music consists mainly of brief sketches, with a psychedelic folk vibe that evokes sunshine and wide-open spaces. The closest he comes to sounding like the mother band is the expansive cover of 'Hard Sun' by obscure Canadian singer-songwriter Indio, which includes backing vocals by Corin Tucker of Sleater-Kinney.

It was four years before Vedder released another solo album, and it was another curveball. *Ukulele Songs* (2011) is exactly what it says on the tin: a collection of songs played on the instrument so beloved of YouTube singers. It's a fun but slight album. Whether you like the ukulele or you hate it, this album is unlikely to change your opinion.

A decade later, Vedder returned to film work with *Flag Day* (2021): the soundtrack to another Sean Penn movie. Most of his songs are collaborations with Academy-award-winning Irish singer-songwriter Glen Hansard, and on two songs, Eddie sings with his daughter Olivia Vedder. In 2022 he released his first *proper* solo album *Earthling*, which featured Red Hot Chili Peppers alumni Josh Klinghoffer and Chad Smith, and also a spot for none other than Elton John: not bad for the man who claimed to hate fame and everything that came with it.

## Stone Gossard

Gossard was the first Pearl Jam member to go solo, releasing the album *Bayleaf* in 2001, followed by *Moonlander* in 2008. In 2021, he teamed with singer-songwriter Mason Jennings for the project *Painted Shield*. But by far his most essential work outside of Pearl Jam was as guitarist for the Seattle band Brad, who released five albums between 1993 and 2012. Brad was not a vanity side-project, but an independent creative unit, highly recommended to fans of softer alt-rock. Their second album *Interiors* (1997) is a good place to start. The band is currently inactive due to the tragic death of singer Shawn Smith (from heart complications instead of drugs, for a change).

## Jeff Ament

Ament is the king of side projects, having recorded with three other bands. Three Fish released two albums, in 1996 and 1999; Tres Mts. released one album in 2011, and RNDM released two albums, in 2012 and 2016. In 2008, Ament also released a solo album called *Tone*, which was recorded over 12 years.

## Mike McCready

McCready played guitar for Seattle band The Rockfords, who released one self-titled album in 2000. He has also played on songs by the bands Walking Papers and Levee Walkers, whose other members include Guns N' Roses bassist Duff McKagan, and Screaming Trees drummer Barrett Martin.

But McCready's most essential side project – indeed, the most essential side project of any Pearl Jam member – is Mad Season. This supergroup was formed in 1994 after McCready met bassist John Baker Saunders while in rehab. They recruited Martin and Alice In Chains vocalist Layne Stanley, and released the album *Above* in 1995. This album is a masterpiece – a sinuous, sensual slice of dark blues rock that sounds unlike any of the members' main bands. Mark Lanegan adds vocals to some songs, making this easily the most high-powered grunge supergroup since Temple Of The Dog. Saunders died in 1999 and Stanley in 2002 – both of drug overdoses, so this one album is all we have. That is until 2013 when they released a three-CD edition with songs from their unfinished second album. 2015 also saw the release of the archival *Live At The Moore 1995* album, and a new live tribute featuring McCready, Martin, Chris Cornell, Duff McKagan and the Seattle Symphony Orchestra!

## Matt Cameron

Before he joined Pearl Jam, Cameron played with the bands Skin Yard and Tone Dogs, and of course, he was the drummer for a little band called Soundgarden. I can't imagine that anyone who's read this far into this book doesn't know who Soundgarden are, but if that's you, rectify it immediately! No home should be without *Badmotorfinger* (1991) and *Superunknown* (1994).

During his first few years as a member of Pearl Jam, Cameron also played with Wellwater Conspiracy: a band formed with ex-Monster Magnet guitarist John McBain. They released four albums between 1997 and 2003, the first of which featured ex-Soundgarden bassist Ben Shepherd on vocals. These three also recorded as the band Hater, who released two albums, in 1993 and 2005. Cameron also released a solo album called Cavedweller in 2017.

## Jack Irons

Irons' most notable work outside Pearl Jam is playing on Red Hot Chili Peppers' first good album *The Uplift Mofo Party Plan* (1987). However, his 2004 solo album *Attention Dimension* is worth checking out, as it includes contributions from Gossard, Ament, and Vedder, who sings on a mind-melting cover of Pink Floyd's 'Shine On You Crazy Diamond'.

# The Best of Pearl Jam

Just for fun, I decided to rank all of Pearl Jam's studio albums and compile a list of what are in my opinion their twenty most essential songs. In determining my rankings, I tried to balance my personal tastes with that of fans, critics, radio programmers, and the record-buying public. You'll likely disagree with my rankings. In a year or so when I look back, I'll probably disagree with my own rankings! But at the very least, these lists should provide a budding Pearl Jam fan with some idea of where to direct their attention.

## All Albums Ranked

I am not including *Temple of The Dog* or the compilation *Lost Dogs*, but if I did, *Temple of The Dog* would go after *Yield*, and *Lost Dogs* would go after *Gigaton*.

1. Ten
2. Vs
3. Yield
4. Vitalogy
5. No Code
6. Pearl Jam
7. Gigaton
8. Backspacer
9. Riot Act
10. Binaural
11. Lightning Bolt

# Top 20 Songs

1. Black
2. Alive
3. Yellow Ledbetter
4. Given to Fly
5. Better Man
6. Corduroy
7. Jeremy
8. Rearviewmirror
9. Elderly Woman Behind the Counter In A Small Town
10. Off He Goes
11. Do the Evolution
12. Even Flow
13. Daughter
14. Release
15. State of Love And Trust
16. Who You Arc
17. Love Boat Captain
18. Just Breathe
19. World Wide Suicide
20. Dance of The Clairvoyants

# Bibliography

Anderson, K., *Accidental Revolution: The Story Of Grunge* (St. Martin's Griffin, 2007)

Arnold, G., *Route 666: On The Road To Nirvana* (Picador, 1993)

Azerrad, M., *Our Band Could Be Your Life: Scenes From The American Indie Underground 1981-1991* (Back Bay Books, 2001)

Basham, D., 'Pearl Jam's Ament probes childhood with 'Seems'' (MTV News Online, 3 May 2000)

Crowe, C., 'Five against the world' (Rolling Stone, 28 October 1993)

DeRogatis, J., *Milk It!* (Da Capo Press, 2003)

Dolan, J. (Ed.), *Pearl Jam: Rolling Stone Special Collectors Edition* (Time Books Inc., 2017)

Garbarini, V., 'All for one' (Guitar World Magazine, March 1998)

Hiatt, B., 'Pearl Jam to release new LP in 2009' (Rolling Stone, 19 February 2009)

Heylin, C., *Babylon's Burning: From Punk To Grunge* (Penguin Books, 2007)

Hilburn, R., 'All revved up (as usual)' (L.A. Times, 20 November 1994)

Hyden, S., 'The best Pearl Jam songs of all time, ranked' (Uproxx.com, 22 November 2019)

Larkin, C., (Ed.), *The Guinness Who's Who Of Indie And New Wave (2nd Edition)* (Guinness Publishing, 1995)

Light, A., 'Pearl Jam's perfect 'Ten'' (MSN Music, 10 April 2009)

Moon, T., 'Calling off the crusades' (Philadelphia Inquirer, 8 February 1998)

Neely, K., *Five Against One: The Pearl Jam Story* (Ebury Press, 1999)

Peterson, C., *Screaming Life* (HarperCollinsWest, 1995)

Reid, G., 'Eddie Vedder: Grunge control' (New Zealand Herald, 6 November 2002)

Reimink, T., 'Q&A with Pearl Jam's Mike McCready' (The Grand Rapids Press, 18 May, 2006)

Tannenbaum, R., 'Rebels without a pause' (George, July 2000)

True, E., *Live Through This: American Rock Music In The Nineties* (Virgin Books, 2001)

Weisbard, E. 'Ten past *Ten*' (Spin, August 2001)

Wheeler, B., 'Vedder talks *Backspacer* track by track' (The Globe And Mail, 16 September, 2009)

WM3.org. 'Echols contributes to new Pearl Jam album' (www.wm3.org, 4 May 2006)

Yarm, M., *Everybody Loves Our Town: A History of Grunge* (Faber & Faber, 2011)

# On Track series

Alan Parsons Project – Steve Swift 978-1-78952-154-2
Tori Amos – Lisa Torem 978-1-78952-142-9
Asia – Peter Braidis 978-1-78952-099-6
Badfinger – Robert Day-Webb 978-1-878952-176-4
Barclay James Harvest – Keith and Monica Domone 978-1-78952-067-5
The Beatles – Andrew Wild 978-1-78952-009-5
The Beatles Solo 1969-1980 – Andrew Wild 978-1-78952-030-9
Blue Oyster Cult – Jacob Holm-Lupo 978-1-78952-007-1
Blur – Matt Bishop – 978-178952-164-1
Marc Bolan and T.Rex – Peter Gallagher 978-1-78952-124-5
Kate Bush – Bill Thomas 978-1-78952-097-2
Camel – Hamish Kuzminski 978-1-78952-040-8
Caravan – Andy Boot 978-1-78952-127-6
Cardiacs – Eric Benac 978-1-78952-131-3
Eric Clapton Solo – Andrew Wild 978-1-78952-141-2
The Clash – Nick Assirati 978-1-78952-077-4
Crosby, Stills and Nash – Andrew Wild 978-1-78952-039-2
The Damned – Morgan Brown 978-1-78952-136-8
Deep Purple and Rainbow 1968-79 – Steve Pilkington 978-1-78952-002-6
Dire Straits – Andrew Wild 978-1-78952-044-6
The Doors – Tony Thompson 978-1-78952-137-5
Dream Theater – Jordan Blum 978-1-78952-050-7
Electric Light Orchestra – Barry Delve 978-1-78952-152-8
Elvis Costello and The Attractions – Georg Purvis 978-1-78952-129-0
Emerson Lake and Palmer – Mike Goode 978-1-78952-000-2
Fairport Convention – Kevan Furbank 978-1-78952-051-4
Peter Gabriel – Graeme Scarfe 978-1-78952-138-2
Genesis – Stuart MacFarlane 978-1-78952-005-7
Gentle Giant – Gary Steel 978-1-78952-058-3
Gong – Kevan Furbank 978-1-78952-082-8
Hall and Oates – Ian Abrahams 978-1-78952-167-2
Hawkwind – Duncan Harris 978-1-78952-052-1
Peter Hammill – Richard Rees Jones 978-1-78952-163-4
Roy Harper – Opher Goodwin 978-1-78952-130-6
Jimi Hendrix – Emma Stott 978-1-78952-175-7
The Hollies – Andrew Darlington 978-1-78952-159-7
Iron Maiden – Steve Pilkington 978-1-78952-061-3
Jefferson Airplane – Richard Butterworth 978-1-78952-143-6
Jethro Tull – Jordan Blum 978-1-78952-016-3
Elton John in the 1970s – Peter Kearns 978-1-78952-034-7
The Incredible String Band – Tim Moon 978-1-78952-107-8
Iron Maiden – Steve Pilkington 978-1-78952-061-3
Judas Priest – John Tucker 978-1-78952-018-7

Kansas – Kevin Cummings 978-1-78952-057-6
The Kinks – Martin Hutchinson 978-1-78952-172-6
Korn – Matt Karpe 978-1-78952-153-5
Led Zeppelin – Steve Pilkington 978-1-78952-151-1
Level 42 – Matt Philips 978-1-78952-102-3
Little Feat – 978-1-78952-168-9
Aimee Mann – Jez Rowden 978-1-78952-036-1
Joni Mitchell – Peter Kearns 978-1-78952-081-1
The Moody Blues – Geoffrey Feakes 978-1-78952-042-2
Motorhead – Duncan Harris 978-1-78952-173-3
Mike Oldfield – Ryan Yard 978-1-78952-060-6
Opeth – Jordan Blum 978-1-78-952-166-5
Tom Petty – Richard James 978-1-78952-128-3
Porcupine Tree – Nick Holmes 978-1-78952-144-3
Queen – Andrew Wild 978-1-78952-003-3
Radiohead – William Allen 978-1-78952-149-8
Renaissance – David Detmer 978-1-78952-062-0
The Rolling Stones 1963-80 – Steve Pilkington 978-1-78952-017-0
The Smiths and Morrissey – Tommy Gunnarsson 978-1-78952-140-5
Status Quo the Frantic Four Years – Richard James 978-1-78952-160-3
Steely Dan – Jez Rowden 978-1-78952-043-9
Steve Hackett – Geoffrey Feakes 978-1-78952-098-9
Thin Lizzy – Graeme Stroud 978-1-78952-064-4
Toto – Jacob Holm-Lupo 978-1-78952-019-4
U2 – Eoghan Lyng 978-1-78952-078-1
UFO – Richard James 978-1-78952-073-6
The Who – Geoffrey Feakes 978-1-78952-076-7
Roy Wood and the Move – James R Turner 978-1-78952-008-8
Van Der Graaf Generator – Dan Coffey 978-1-78952-031-6
Yes – Stephen Lambe 978-1-78952-001-9
Frank Zappa 1966 to 1979 – Eric Benac 978-1-78952-033-0
Warren Zevon – Peter Gallagher 978-1-78952-170-2
10CC – Peter Kearns 978-1-78952-054-5

## Decades Series

The Bee Gees in the 1960s – Andrew Mon Hughes et al 978-1-78952-148-1
The Bee Gees in the 1970s – Andrew Mon Hughes et al 978-1-78952-179-5
Black Sabbath in the 1970s – Chris Sutton 978-1-78952-171-9
Britpop – Peter Richard Adams and Matt Pooler 978-1-78952-169-6
Alice Cooper in the 1970s – Chris Sutton 978-1-78952-104-7
Curved Air in the 1970s – Laura Shenton 978-1-78952-069-9
Bob Dylan in the 1980s – Don Klees 978-1-78952-157-3
Fleetwood Mac in the 1970s – Andrew Wild 978-1-78952-105-4
Focus in the 1970s – Stephen Lambe 978-1-78952-079-8
Free and Bad Company in the 1970s – John Van der Kiste 978-1-78952-178-8

Genesis in the 1970s – Bill Thomas 978178952-146-7
George Harrison in the 1970s – Eoghan Lyng 978-1-78952-174-0
Marillion in the 1980s – Nathaniel Webb 978-1-78952-065-1
Mott the Hoople and Ian Hunter in the 1970s – John Van der Kiste
978-1-78-952-162-7
Pink Floyd In The 1970s – Georg Purvis 978-1-78952-072-9
Tangerine Dream in the 1970s – Stephen Palmer 978-1-78952-161-0
The Sweet in the 1970s – Darren Johnson 978-1-78952-139-9
Uriah Heep in the 1970s – Steve Pilkington 978-1-78952-103-0
Yes in the 1980s – Stephen Lambe with David Watkinson 978-1-78952-125-2

## On Screen series
Carry On… – Stephen Lambe 978-1-78952-004-0
David Cronenberg – Patrick Chapman 978-1-78952-071-2
Doctor Who: The David Tennant Years – Jamie Hailstone 978-1-78952-066-8
James Bond – Andrew Wild – 978-1-78952-010-1
Monty Python – Steve Pilkington 978-1-78952-047-7
Seinfeld Seasons 1 to 5 – Stephen Lambe 978-1-78952-012-5

## Other Books
1967: A Year In Psychedelic Rock – Kevan Furbank 978-1-78952-155-9
1970: A Year In Rock – John Van der Kiste 978-1-78952-147-4
1973: The Golden Year of Progressive Rock 978-1-78952-165-8
Babysitting A Band On The Rocks – G.D. Praetorius 978-1-78952-106-1
Eric Clapton Sessions – Andrew Wild 978-1-78952-177-1
Derek Taylor: For Your Radioactive Children – Andrew Darlington
978-1-78952-038-5
The Golden Road: The Recording History of The Grateful Dead – John Kilbride
978-1-78952-156-6
Iggy and The Stooges On Stage 1967-1974 – Per Nilsen 978-1-78952-101-6
Jon Anderson and the Warriors – the road to Yes – David Watkinson
978-1-78952-059-0
Nu Metal: A Definitive Guide – Matt Karpe 978-1-78952-063-7
Tommy Bolin: In and Out of Deep Purple – Laura Shenton 978-1-78952-070-5
Maximum Darkness – Deke Leonard 978-1-78952-048-4
Maybe I Should've Stayed In Bed – Deke Leonard 978-1-78952-053-8
The Twang Dynasty – Deke Leonard 978-1-78952-049-1

*and many more to come!*

**Would you like to write for Sonicbond Publishing?**
We are mainly a music publisher, but we also occasionally publish in other genres including film and television. At Sonicbond Publishing we are always on the look-out for authors, particularly for our two main series, On Track and Decades.

Mixing fact with in depth analysis, the On Track series examines the entire recorded work of a particular musical artist or group. All genres are considered from easy listening and jazz to 60s soul to 90s pop, via rock and metal.

The Decades series singles out a particular decade in an artist or group's history and focuses on that decade in more detail than may be allowed in the On Track series.

While professional writing experience would, of course, be an advantage, the most important qualification is to have real enthusiasm and knowledge of your subject. First-time authors are welcomed, but the ability to write well in English is essential.

Sonicbond Publishing has distribution throughout Europe and North America, and all our books are also published in E-book form. Authors will be paid a royalty based on sales of their book. Further details about our books are available from www.sonicbondpublishing.com. To contact us, complete the contact form there or email info@sonicbondpublishing.co.uk